POLICY AND PRACTICE IN EDUCATION

NUMBER TWO

ENHANCING QUALITY IN TEACHER EDUCATION

POLICY AND PRACTICE IN EDUCATION

POLICY AND PRACTICE IN EDUCATION

EDITORS

GORDON KIRK *AND* ROBERT GLAISTER

ENHANCING QUALITY IN TEACHER EDUCATION

Gordon Kirk

DUNEDIN ACADEMIC PRESS

EDINBURGH

Published by
Dunedin Academic Press Ltd
8 Albany Street
Edinburgh EH1 3QB

ISBN 1 903765 01 3

© 2000 Gordon Kirk

British Library Cataloguing in Publication Data

A catalogue record for this book is available from the British Library

Typeset by Trinity Typing, Coldstream
Printed in Great Britain by Polestar AUP Aberdeen Limited

CONTENTS

EDITORIAL INTRODUCTION

Education is now widely regarded as having a key contribution to make to national prosperity and to the well-being of the community. Arguably, of all forms of investment in the public good, it deserves the highest priority. Given the importance of education, it is natural that it should be the focus of widespread public interest and that the effectiveness and responsiveness of the educational service should be of vital concern to politicians, teachers and other professionals, parents and members of the general public. If anything, the establishment of Scotland's parliament, which has already affirmed education as a key priority, will witness an intensification of public interest in the nature and direction of educational policy and the changing practices in the schools. This series of books on *Policy and Practice in Education* seeks to support the public and professional discussion of education in Scotland.

In recent years there have been significant changes in every aspect of education in Scotland. The series seeks to counter the tendency for such changes to be under-documented and to take place without sufficient critical scrutiny. While it will focus on changes of policy and practice in Scotland, it will seek to relate developments to the wider international debate on education.

Each volume in the series will focus on a particular aspect of education, reflecting upon the past, analysing the present, and contemplating the future. The contributing authors are all well established and bring to their writing an intimate knowledge of their field, as well as the capacity to offer a readable and authoritative analysis of policies and practices.

The author of this volume, the second in the series, is Professor Gordon Kirk, Principal of Moray House Institute of Education from 1981 to 1998, and since 1998 Dean of the Faculty of Education at the University of Edinburgh, following the merger of Moray House with the University.

Professor Gordon Kirk   Dr Robert T D Glaister
Faculty of Education   School of Education
The University of Edinburgh   The Open University

ACKNOWLEDGEMENTS

The preparation of a book for publication depends on the assistance, support and goodwill of very many people. This book is no exception. I therefore express my indebtedness to fellow members of the Scottish Teacher Education Committee and colleagues at Moray House and in its new home in the Faculty of Education of The University of Edinburgh for the many conversations which helped to crystallise ideas; to Dr Bob Glaister, co-editor of the series, for his comments on an earlier draft; to David Fairgrieve and Hazel Robertson of the Moray House Library and Information Centre, who responded willingly to numerous calls for help; to Dr David Jenkins for his eagle-eyed proof-reading; to Mary Speed, as ever, for her patience and skill in word-processing the text into its final form; to the Editor of *Scottish Educational Review* for permission to draw on my article in a recent issue of the journal in writing chapter 1; and to the Editor of the *Times Educational Supplement Scotland* for agreeing that I could elaborate, in chapters 2, 3 and 4, ideas that first appeared on the pages of that newspaper. Finally, I record my indebtedness to my wife, Jane, for her interest and support, and much else besides.

CHAPTER 1

THE NEW INSTITUTIONAL CONTEXT

Introduction

Teacher education in Scotland was traditionally provided by specialist monotechnic institutions. Indeed, the monotechnic approach was officially endorsed by a national committee of enquiry as recently as 1986. Now, however, all of Scotland's teacher education is located within universities. Why did Scotland persist with specialist teacher education institutions? What were the factors which led to the incorporation of teacher education within universities? And how will teacher education be influenced by its new institutional context? These are the questions to be addressed in this chapter.

The Monotechnic Tradition

The location of teacher education in specialist institutions devoted mainly, if not exclusively, to that purpose was a significant feature of Scotland's educational tradition. Even although teacher education had been incorporated within universities in other parts of the world, for example in North America, in Australia, and in England, Scotland retained its system of independent colleges of education, which formed a separate sector of higher education with its own financial arrangements, patterns of accountability, procedures for course management, approval and validation, and operating within a distinctive legal and administrative framework.

There are three explanations for the retention of the monotechnic system long after it had been discarded elsewhere. Firstly, it was maintained that the Secretary of State for Scotland, who was responsible to parliament for the quality of the education provided by the schools, had to control the professional education of teachers. That responsibility could not be discharged if teacher education was based in universities, for these fell within the jurisdiction of a separate minister at the Department of Education and Science based in London.

Secondly, the Scottish Office was committed to the establishment of three separate sectors of higher education: the universities, the central institutions, and the colleges of education. In England, a "binary" system of higher education had been introduced in the mid-60s, with universities on the one hand and non-university institutions on the other. However, while there were some areas of study that were peculiar to the universities — for example, medicine — the two systems developed side-by-side with frequently overlapping provision. That duplication was justified on the grounds that the "public" sector was more amenable to ministerial influence than the university sector. The Scottish Office was concerned to avoid such duplication of provision. The universities were seen as having a distinctive function, in line with universities elsewhere in the UK. The central institutions were expected to provide specialised vocational education. Where that overlapped with provision in the universities it was considered to be more directly attuned to the needs of industry and commerce and, moreover, it could be provided more cheaply than in the universities. Teacher education institutions were thought to have a distinctive function not provided by the other two sectors. In Scotland, therefore, the structure of higher education was thought to be functionally differentiated and the national governance of the three systems called for separate administrative and financial arrangements.

Thirdly, whether or not because of the separate political control, there was a strong professional consensus that teacher education should be provided in separate establishments. Two examples of that professional consensus might be invoked. Firstly, the Advisory Council report, *Training of Teachers* (SED, 1946), addressed the question of the most appropriate institutional context for teacher education: should the training of teachers be taken over by the universities? The committee adduced several advantages for university control: it would enhance the status of the profession; it would attract stronger entrants to teaching; it would establish an all-graduate profession; it would enable all students to have the advantages of participation in the life of a university; and it would be easier to integrate students' general education with their professional preparation. Members of the Advisory Council were "not convinced of the soundness of these claims". They maintained that the training of teachers was an integral part of the state system and that it would be undemocratic if responsibility were to transfer to "a private body, many of whose members are not in close touch with the schools". Besides, it was felt that training institutions were geographically separate from the universities so that the advantages claimed in favour of integration would not be realised. Finally, to insist that all teachers should require to be graduates was to exalt the intellectual at the expense of other personal qualities, with the result that the schools would be "impoverished" by not having the benefit of those who brought a wider range of skills to the profession, as well as experience of industry and commerce.

The Council was also opposed to the transference of teacher education to the universities because there appeared to be no professional support for it. Sixteen of the seventeen witnesses who expressed a view were opposed to the principle of graduation for all primary teachers; and thirty-four of thirty-nine who expressed a definite view on the matter were in favour of placing control of teacher training in the hands of *ad hoc* training authorities rather than universities.

However, the primary reason for disagreeing to the transfer of teacher education to the universities was that the Council believed that teacher education should be conducted in special "Institutes of Education", which would be centres of educational study, research and professional development, "a resort for teachers and the focal point of the educational activities of the province". The institutes would maintain close working relationships with schools; there would be transfer of staff between schools and the institutes; collaboration would take place in research and curriculum development; and the institutes would become major centres of support for the work of the schools.

There is no doubt that the Advisory Council's strong endorsement of separate teacher education institutions was influenced by the view that the inclusion of teacher education within universities would "endanger the fulfilment of their true cultural mission". While the Advisory Council therefore reflected a professional consensus in urging that specialist provision be continued for teacher education, one of the principal grounds for its conclusion was that teacher education studies were judged unworthy of inclusion in the university curriculum.

The second example of the professional consensus on the institutional context of teacher education occurred forty years later, when the Scottish Tertiary Education Advisory Council (STEAC) (SED, 1985) addressed the same issue. Established to examine the relationships between the separate sectors of higher education, STEAC received evidence which was strongly critical of the teacher education institutions. For example, it was argued that in small institutions staff were academically isolated; the costs of administration and infrastructure were unduly high; and there was substantial unused accommodation. Besides, there appeared to be no evidence for the validity of the proposition that education is best undertaken in monotechnic institutions. Despite the volume of opposition to the continuation of a separate teacher education sector, the committee nevertheless recommended that teacher education should be retained in separate institutions. What arguments persuaded them to reach that conclusion?

Firstly, there was a fear of academic drift. The incorporation of teacher education within universities would lead to "an excessively academic approach". While that might nurture the students intellectually, it would not necessarily help them to become better teachers. Secondly, if teacher education became the responsibility of the universities and therefore of a separate minister, the government's control of teacher education would be significantly reduced. That conclusion was reached despite three pieces of evidence to the contrary: ministers retained certain controls in medical education — for example, the level of intake — despite its location in universities; teacher education was integrated into universities elsewhere, without any apparent diminution in government control; and the Secretary of State had statutory authority to approve all teacher education programmes. Thirdly, members of STEAC feared that the transfer would significantly increase the resources required for training teachers because of additional salary and superannuation costs. These were already high because of the more favourable staff:student ratio which was required mainly to accommodate placement supervision arrangements. Fourthly, it was acknowledged that the incorporation of a college of education in another institution would not necessarily mean integration, in the sense of enabling potential teachers to rub shoulders with those destined for other occupations. Where a college of education became part of a university but remained on its existing site, students and staff would continue to be segregated.

Fifthly, STEAC was impressed by the unanimity of view expressed by the principals in their oral and supplementary personal evidence. They offered two principal justifications for the continuation of the monotechnic system. The first of these was educational:

> There is ample room (in higher education) for institutions which make no claim to comprehensiveness of academic or intellectual coverage, but which have a distinctive and specialised professional function to perform. The centrality of that preoccupation with professional activity does not weaken the institution: on the contrary, it is the source of the institution's strength, providing a focus for individual, inter-departmental and institutional activity. Besides, the relatively restricted range of its academic and professional coverage helps to maintain the quality of the academic environment, to sharpen the sense of institutional purpose, and to provide a powerful source of student motivation. (Kirk, 1985)

The second justification concerned the question of academic and professional control. It was strongly maintained that the incorporation of teacher education within universities

> would entail the transference of decision-making on courses and related matters from those who have the necessary expertise and experience to make relevant professional judgements to those who lack that experience ... and who have not grasped the distinction between academic accomplishment and the capacity for intelligent professional action. If the college of education function were to be absorbed within a larger institution professional decision-making would be even further distanced from the professions with whom colleges of education work very closely and the full professionalisation of teaching and related activities would be inhibited. (Kirk, 1984)

STEAC concluded its strategic analysis of higher education by endorsing the monotechnic principle in these words: "the standard of teacher training in Scotland will, in our view, be best preserved by its concentration in thriving specialist establishments with a common sense of purpose".

Following an extensive period of consultation, which was dominated by the teacher education issue, the Secretary of State announced to parliament in July 1986 that teacher training "should continue to be provided in specialist institutions", although there was a need to reduce the system from seven colleges to five on account of the significant evidence of over-capacity. Clearly, one of the key factors influencing the Secretary of State was the need for "a fairly wide geographical spread of provision". It was for that reason that, while the number of colleges would be reduced, none of the existing centres would be closed: Dundee and Aberdeen Colleges would merge to form the Northern College, and Dunfermline College of Physical Education, which would become the single centre for the provision of physical education courses, would merge with Moray House College of Education.

Institutional Strategic Alliances

Subsequent to the endorsement of the monotechnic principle by STEAC there have been significant developments, with each of the colleges forming a strategic alliance with a university. In the first of these, in 1989, Moray House became an associated college of Heriot-Watt University. The following year, Craigie College of Education became the School of Education of the University of Strathclyde. However, when Jordanhill College of Education merged with the University of Strathclyde in 1992 to become its Faculty of Education, Craigie College of Education entered discussion with the University of Paisley and in 1993 became the Faculty of Education of that university. After several years operating as an associated college of Heriot-Watt University, Moray House merged with the University of Edinburgh in 1998; St Andrew's College of Education merged with the University of Glasgow in 1999; and in 2000 Northern College of Education is scheduled to "demerge", with the Aberdeen campus becoming the Faculty of Education of the University of Aberdeen, and the Dundee campus becoming the Faculty of Education of the University of Dundee. In little more than a decade, then, there has been a radical transformation in the institutional context of teacher education. What were the reasons for that transformation?

The Aftermath of STEAC

In a detailed study, Kirk (1997) has argued that the STEAC settlement was more concerned to reconcile conflicting political pressures than to determine the strategic development of the teacher education sector. The fragility of that settlement was evidenced in a number of ways. The first of these was ministerial uncertainty. While affirming that teacher education should continue in separate establishments, Malcolm Rifkind indicated under questioning in the House of Commons that he had made that decision "in principle, while not ruling out entirely the possibility of some other arrangement if circumstances appeared to warrant it". That reply revealed the Secretary of State's own view that teacher education centres should be integrated with other institutions of higher education. In the same debate, the Secretary of State actually referred to experience elsewhere in the UK where "teacher training institutions were attached to other establishments". He clearly did not wish to rule out the possibility that at some future date that approach might be required also in Scotland. Furthermore, again in the same debate, Malcolm Rifkind indicated that he would "review the position again next year in the light of progress made" in the disposal of surplus accommodation.

The STEAC settlement was also suspect in the sense that many of the arguments adduced in favour of the monotechnic principle were unconvincing. For example, members of STEAC must have been well aware that in other parts of the world, even in England, teacher education had been incorporated into universities. Besides, there could be no reasonable grounds for believing that the incorporation of teacher education within universities would lead to "academic drift" for the simple reason that the Secretary of State approved teacher education programmes and therefore would have every opportunity to prevent any weakening of the professional dimension in teacher education. It appeared, indeed, that a powerful committee had simply acquiesced in the rhetoric of the proponents of the monotechnic principle.

Given the weakness of the arguments, it was hardly surprising that many respected bodies expressed opposition to the central STEAC recommendation on colleges of education. These included the Council for National Academic Awards, the technological central institutions, the Church of Scotland's Education Committee, the Convention of Scottish Local Authorities, the Association of Directors of Education in Scotland, the National Association of Schoolmasters/Union of Women Teachers, and the university departments of education. Indeed, the last named were "sceptical about the desirability of the largely monotechnic nature of the colleges as at present organised", on the grounds that it would reinforce "a narrow conception of professionalism confined to schooling and classroom competence". They concluded: "It would be a greater service to the educational system and to the colleges themselves if they were to be more closely and organically linked with universities or central institutions, rather than being marginalised as at present." The existence of a strong body of contrary opinion clearly indicated that the confidence that had been placed by a national committee in the monotechnic principle might not be entirely justified.

Even after STEAC, colleges continued to be at the mercy of fluctuating demands and had all the vulnerability of being dependent on a single major activity. Moreover, the scope for diversification was extremely restricted. The Scottish Office commitment to a differentiated system of higher education made it impossible for the colleges of education to enter lines of activity that already were being developed in the other two sectors of higher education. The vulnerability of the colleges, therefore, was reinforced by the fragility of the STEAC settlement: far from resolving the perennial difficulties of the teacher education sector, it left them as isolated and exposed as ever.

The institutional uncertainty following STEAC was accentuated by the review of teacher education at the University of Stirling. Noting that the teacher education based there was anomalous, STEAC, in order to show confidence in its own judgement that teacher education should be provided in monotechnic institutions, recommended that a review of the Stirling Education Department should be undertaken. The review could not have been more flattering. It concluded:

> The evidence of our review showed that the Department of Education at the University of Stirling produces well trained, enthusiastic probationer teachers; provides highly regarded, innovative in-service training courses; and has undertaken valuable classroom-based research. Overall, the Department makes a considerable contribution to the quality of teaching, both in its immediate vicinity and throughout the country as a whole. (SED, 1988)

The department at Stirling was described as offering courses of high quality in a relatively cost-effective method. Far from leading to a discontinuation of teacher education at the University of Stirling, the review positively endorsed that training and therefore strongly reinforced the view, contrary to the recommendation of STEAC, that teacher education could flourish within a university context. This finding, so counter to the basic philosophy of the STEAC report, served to invalidate the STEAC settlement and to create an even greater degree of uncertainty in the college sector.

Mergermania

Another factor leading to a destabilised system was the amount of interest taken in and attention devoted to mergers and the possibility of mergers. There were several manifestations of this "mergermania". The first of these was a pamphlet produced by Bill Turmeau, Principal of Napier Polytechnic. In a plan intended "to increase the efficiency and effectiveness of higher education in Scotland" he proposed that there should be a substantial reduction in the number of individual higher education institutions from twenty-five to, at most, ten. On the assumption that the optimum number of students was 5,000, there was a need for widespread institutional amalgamations. The Turmeau plan envisaged four major groupings of institutions, with the smaller institutions becoming part of larger non-university federations. Secondly, Michael Forsyth, Minister for Education, in his address to the Principals of Centrally-funded Colleges in 1989, devoted a substantial section to institutional collaboration, making specific reference to mergers involving colleges of education. Thirdly, in 1991 the Universities' Funding Council Scottish Committee (Universities' Funding Council, 1991) produced a report on the criteria for assessing merger proposals in higher education. Teacher education institutions were singled out for special mention, it being asserted that "the committee does not see any positive advantages in colleges of education remaining essentially monotechnic institutions". Finally, the Convener of the Committee of Scottish Higher Education Principals (COSHEP), the body that was supposed to speak for all of the institutions, publicly intimated that the difficulties facing higher education were bound to be "particularly acute in Scotland's smaller higher education institutions. With more cuts to come there was a danger that some of these colleges would have to sacrifice their autonomy and merge with a bigger institution."

The prevailing insecurity was intensified by the threatened demise of the Council for National Academic Awards (CNAA), which validated the programmes in several of the colleges of education. In 1988 the polytechnics won their independence from local authority control and became autonomous higher education institutions. It was predictable, given this significant development, that these institutions would wish to mark their autonomy by being able to award their own degrees. At the time, the polytechnics accounted for about 85% of CNAA's work. If the polytechnics became degree-awarding bodies, they would have no further need for the CNAA and the future of that organisation would be in jeopardy. In that event, the polytechnics might see themselves as the natural bodies to validate the programmes of those institutions which did not have degree-awarding powers. Such a change would have the effect of locking the smaller colleges into the non-university sector. That development certainly seemed to be a central aim of government policy: by strongly supporting the establishment of the Conference of Scottish Centrally-funded Colleges, the Scottish Office hoped to retain significant control over a major sector of higher education.

Finally, the uncertainty was reinforced by the change of policy in 1987 whereby the government appeared to adopt an arm's length approach to institutions. Retreating from the micro-management of the system, the Scottish Office sought to place pressure on institutions to be self-reliant, innovative and independent. The goal was a system of higher education that was genuinely diverse and in which the various institutions openly competed for students and for funds. Ministers reinforced this vision. For example, the Secretary of State himself asserted in May 1990 that "competition — or, to put it another way, choice for the consumer — is an essential and desirable element of a healthy service industry such as your own". And the Minister for Education, Michael Forsyth, was equally candid:

> The consistent thread running through all our policies for the grant-aided colleges is to emphasise that your future is in your own hands. I believe we are creating a climate which is bracing, healthy and

even stimulating. The fittest colleges will be able to go from strength to strength, and the remedy for the others will be in their own hands.

Understandably, smaller institutions, with no scope for diversification, might well feel threatened in such a hostile environment. Indeed, one commentator described them as being "as exposed as Spartan babies".

The Repatriation of the Scottish Universities

At the time of the STEAC review the weight of university opinion was strongly against repatriation. The universities saw themselves as British institutions. There was a significant cross-border flow of students; a substantial proportion of staff were the graduates of universities south of the border; there were UK salary scales; and there was a UK funding body, the University Grants Committee (UGC). The universities regarded it as crucial to retain membership of the UK — and, indeed, the wider international — academic community, not only to protect standards, but also to ensure continued access to funding from the research councils. Besides, the existence of such UK-wide institutions as the Open University and the CNAA, and the fact that they were the responsibility of a single UK minister, served to reinforce the standing of the universities as British rather than as Scottish institutions. However, the growth of devolutionary sentiment throughout the '80s, partly in response to an unpopular Tory government, whose legitimacy in Scotland was questioned, and partly out of a growing lack of confidence in the UGC, strengthened the case for repatriation. Moreover, when the binary system in England and Wales was scheduled to be dismantled and a single mechanism to oversee all higher education in England was mooted, repatriation became inevitable. That was formally completed with the establishment in 1992 of the Scottish Higher Education Funding Council (SHEFC). While that created a separate higher education system in Scotland, it nevertheless allowed universities in Scotland to retain strong links with their counterparts in England and Wales: the Research Assessment Exercise (RAE) would be undertaken on a UK basis; all institutions would have equal access to the research councils for funding; and the Higher Education Quality Council (HEQC) would carry responsibility for quality assurance and quality control on a UK basis. It appeared, therefore, that, as far as the universities were concerned, they could retain their British connections while, at the same time, operating firmly within a Scottish framework.

The principal effect of the Act of 1992 was to create a structure of higher education in Scotland based on the universities. All institutions came to have the same constitutional relationship to the Funding Council and all operated within the same framework of financial accountability. That meant that the principal justification for a separate system of colleges of education was removed: all institutions of higher education in Scotland were now the responsibility of the Secretary of State for Scotland. Moreover, once the principals began to organise themselves as the Committee for Scottish Higher Education Principals, some of the misconceptions and stereotypes of the past were mistrusted and discarded. For its part, the SHEFC sought to create a culture of collaboration by allocating substantial sums to enable institutions to manage the financial and other costs of creating strategic academic alliances. In such a context, it was highly likely that, given their vulnerability, teacher education institutions would seek to form alliances with universities.

Financial Pressures

Higher education as a whole was obliged to operate within tight fiscal restraints, but for the teacher education institutions the financial environment throughout the late '80s and early '90s became increasingly hostile. In order to retain the level of grant reduction within manageable proportions certain colleges had to be "safety-netted". That was interpreted by other institutions as a "tax", for it meant that money that could have gone to the institutions generally was being used to retain in existence colleges that were thought to have passed the point of financial viability. SHEFC was therefore under pressure to withdraw safety-netting and an announcement was made to that effect in 1996. The reductions in income in the three safety-netted institutions were as follows:

	1995/96	1996/97	1997/98
Moray House	- 1.0%	-2.6%	-5.3%
Northern	-1.0%	-2.3%	-6.1%
St Andrew's	-1.0%	-4.6%	-0.8%

The reduction in income from SHEFC was paralleled by a drop in income from other sources, particularly when funds which had once been reserved for in-service work in the shape of specific grants were no longer ear-marked but included within the overall budget of local authorities. In the face of such financial difficulties, the teacher education institutions had to work hard to maintain morale at a time when it appeared as though the community had lost confidence in their work. A wholly disproportionate amount of management time was devoted to the maintenance of the institutions' financial viability. Faced with the prospect of even gloomier financial scenarios, these institutions were bound to question whether the price of institutional autonomy and independence was a price worth paying. Moreover, it became apparent that, by joining with larger institutions, there could be significant economies of scale and efficiencies in teaching, in the provision of services, in estates, and in other ways. The colleges were therefore bound to question the wisdom of opposing efficiencies which appeared to constitute the only means of protecting the quality of their work.

The Educational Case for Merger

A range of educational considerations also exerted pressure towards merger. The most important of these concerned the pressure on institutions to enhance the quality of their work. In the system of academic accountability established under the new Funding Council teaching and research were exposed to external scrutiny. The Teaching Quality Assessment process permitted an independent check to be made on the standards and quality of the educational experience institutions offered. The report of the Teaching Quality Assessment of Initial Teacher Education in 1995 (SHEFC, 1995) showed that none of the teacher education institutions achieved the highest standard: five of them obtained a rating of "Highly Satisfactory", and one a rating of "Satisfactory". The possibility could not be discounted that the quality of their work might be enhanced in a different institutional setting.

The pressure to enhance research ratings was even stronger, for that directly influenced the income attracted by the institution. Again, in successive Research Assessment Exercises in 1992 and 1996, only one of the teacher education centres achieved the highest rating and that was a centre that was based in a university. Colleges could see that they might be able to enhance their research profile, and achieve the educational and financial advantages of so doing, by forming an alliance with a university.

The advantages of locating teacher education within institutions of higher education were reinforced by the findings of the Dearing/Garrick Committee. Part of that enquiry involved an independent study of teacher education by Sir Stewart Sutherland. His report concluded:

> On academic grounds, I believe that the proposals that I have put forward point inevitably towards the provision of teacher education within a broader intellectual context than can be provided by monotechnics. There are also strong arguments that the student experience in Scotland is likely to be enhanced through being educated in a broader HE context and, indeed, that the staff experience will be strengthened through contact with, or integration into, the research environment of a university. (Sutherland, 1997)

A number of more direct educational advantages were also apparent. Firstly, it was believed that courses would be strengthened if the providers of teacher education were able to draw on the intellectual resources and the internationally recognised excellence of university scholars. If teacher education programmes were open to the criticism that they made insufficient cognitive demands, locating programmes within a university would be a way of strengthening the academic base of initial teacher education and programmes of continuing professional development for teachers. Secondly, greater flexibility would be introduced in recruitment to teaching by increasing the number of "concurrent" courses, in which academic study of a subject or subjects is combined with professional studies and school experience. Thirdly, it was believed that teacher education programmes would be enriched by being located in the research culture promoted by the universities. In this respect, the universities were thought to offer the kind of environment which colleges of education on their own were unable to sustain.

Fourthly, the incorporation of teacher education and related studies within a university environment would contribute significantly to their enhanced professional standing. Teacher education would obtain greater recognition by being located in institutions which trained for the other great professions of medicine, law, engineering and business and commerce. As a consequence, recruitment of both students and staff would be strengthened, and the public perception of teaching and other forms of professional education would be improved once it was recognised that these studies were sufficiently demanding to warrant inclusion within a university curriculum.

Finally, it was believed that locating teacher education within universities would significantly enrich the quality of the educational experience offered to students and the quality of the learning environment for staff. Students would have the benefits of working with those from other backgrounds and destined for other occupations, and would also have access to a range of informal educational opportunities which colleges of education simply could not make available. For their part, staff would have enhanced opportunities for engagement in research and enjoy the educational benefits that come from working in a more intellectually demanding environment.

There were two areas of concern. The first of these was that colleges of education would lose their strong professional orientation. It had always been assumed in colleges of education that their work should certainly be academically demanding in the sense that it should stretch students intellectually. On the other hand, it should also be professionally demanding: it should issue in competent professional performance in schools and other settings. That fear was at least partly allayed by the recognition that universities themselves were major centres of professional education, offering programmes in medicine, engineering, and law. However, there were other ways of protecting the professional orientation of the work of the colleges of education. Teacher education programmes required to be approved of the Secretary of State for Scotland and accredited by the General Teaching Council for Scotland. If the universities wished programmes to retain professional recognition, they would have to accord with the professional expectations of the General Teaching Council and the national guidelines stipulated by the Secretary of State.

A second concern was that members of staff might find themselves under pressure to switch their allegiance from teaching to research. Of course, a university does not polarise activities in that way: it assumes that membership of an institution of higher education imposes two obligations — to teach and to undertake research. While the universities over the years had been funded to undertake research, colleges of education had not, and while the colleges had been developing their research profiles, participation in research was still well below the level assumed to be acceptable for a university. In the various merger discussions, it was acknowledged that there was a need to raise the research profile of the new faculties of education. Nevertheless, it was fully recognised that, certainly initially, the level of participation in research might be lower than might be typical of other faculties, if only because the staff in the former colleges of education had a wider range of obligations. For example, they needed to maintain strong links with schools; they tended to have much higher teaching loads; they were encouraged to participate in national and local curriculum development work; and they were expected to retain their professional credibility in other ways. However, the inclusion in the new faculties of education of established members of staff of the universities would create a stronger critical mass of research expertise and help to generate a stronger research culture for the work of the former colleges of education.

At the time of the merger discussions educational research came in for serious criticism, mainly because it did not appear to relate directly to the work of teachers in classrooms. Clearly, former college of education staff, who had strong links with schools, were well placed to participate in research that might be of direct benefit to teachers. Accordingly, the expectation that former college of education staff should participate in research did not necessarily entail a retreat from their professional responsibilities. If anything, it would sharpen the professional focus of their work, for it would mean that the staff concerned would be researching into the very processes of teaching and learning that will, at one and the same time, enrich their own teaching and enhance the curriculum development work they undertake with teachers in schools.

It could be argued, of course, that these educational benefits of incorporating teacher education within the university environment were well established and had been fully rehearsed at the time of the STEAC review. Yet, at the time of that review, as has been noted, the colleges of education, with the exception of Jordanhill, vigorously defended their independence. Is the decision, belatedly, to seek affiliation with universities to be seen as a U-turn, the response of cynical opportunists who are prepared to invoke whatever rhetoric best serves personal and institutional self-interest?

The stance of the college of education principals during the STEAC review could be described as self-serving, in the sense that it entailed a rejection of an institutional arrangement which might have secured the long-term viability and well-being of teacher education and related studies. However, during the debate in the mid-80s, the universities showed no interest in incorporating the colleges of education, if only because the evidence suggested that they might well be a financial liability. On the other hand, the heads of the technological central institutions — particularly

Bill Turmeau of Napier and Harry Cuming of Dundee, who was a member of STEAC — would have felt their position to be strengthened if they had been able to incorporate the colleges of education. For their part, the principals of the colleges of education did not see an alliance with a central institution as in any way appropriate: their links with the CIs were practically non-existent, while nearly all of them had associations, sometimes extending over many years, with a university. The college of education principals defended their independence as a counter to possible incorporation by central institutions.

There are therefore three factors which explain the change of attitude on the part of the colleges of education. The first was the intensifying financial pressure. Secondly, the central institution sector of higher education had disappeared, leaving colleges of education with no option but to merge with a university, and in all cases but one, where very special circumstances obtained, mergers have involved established universities. Thirdly, there appears to have been a change in the attitude of the universities to the colleges of education.

The Attitude of the Universities

While the colleges of education were subject to financial and academic pressures which made links with a university an attractive proposition, the universities themselves had to be convinced of the value of incorporating colleges of education. Indeed, universities came to see significant advantages: they could affirm their membership of local communities; they could strengthen their links through the faculties of education with the schools; they would be able to make a more direct contribution to the education of teachers and to the continuing professional development of teachers, not least in the area of subject up-dating, an area of in-service provision for teachers that has been under-developed; and they would have the opportunity to remedy some of the alleged deficiencies of the schools by ensuring that the education of teachers was significantly strengthened. In addition, the creation of faculties of education would enable universities to rationalise a range of education-related activities, such as the Teaching, Learning and Assessment Centre and the Centre for Educational Sociology at Edinburgh, the Department of Adult and Continuing Education and the Centre for Science Education at Glasgow, the Centre for Continuing Education and the Department of Educational Studies at Dundee, and the Centre for Educational Research at Aberdeen. By establishing faculties of education which incorporated the former college of education staff, together with established university staff with expertise in education, universities sought to create strong concentrations of educational expertise. Finally, perhaps more than anything, the incorporation of colleges of education enabled the universities to affirm themselves as integral to Scottish education, a move which had been formalised by the 1992 settlement and has been reinforced by the establishment of the Scottish Parliament in 1999.

The incorporation of the former colleges of education within the universities, therefore, offers the prospect of a significant enhancement of the educational experience of staff and students; it promises richer and more challenging programmes of professional education and of continuing support for teachers; and it brings an end to a period of extreme vulnerability when institutional viability was a subject of perennial concern.

Those now responsible for teacher education, in its new institutional context, are able to devote themselves to the strengthening of programmes, to the enrichment of the educational experience of their students, and to the strengthening of the educational system in general through their research and development activities, while contributing also to the wider work of the universities in which they are now embedded. The benefits of the integration of teacher education within the institutional context of the universities have been summarised as follows:

> What matters, surely, is that the colleges have earned full membership of the university community; that their important work of educating and providing professional support for teachers and related professionals is now located in a richer, a more secure, and a more challenging environment; that the professional values underpinning their work have been endorsed and protected; and that the universities themselves, as they acknowledge, are among the principal beneficiaries. (Kirk, 1999)

CHAPTER 2

THE REFORM OF INITIAL TEACHER EDUCATION

Introduction

The education of teachers is an area of public policy that is not short of stakeholders. The First Minister, who is accountable to Scotland's parliament for education in Scotland, must be able to ensure that teachers undergo the kind of professional preparation that meets the changing needs of the school; the universities are entitled to insist that awards made in their name comply with their academic requirements; the General Teaching Council for Scotland, the custodian of professional standards, has a duty to satisfy itself that those who are registered to teach have completed a programme of study and training that fully meets their professional expectations; teachers in schools need to be assured that their future colleagues will be able to make an effective contribution, even as junior members of a school staff; teacher educators themselves have a special contribution to make to the shaping of the teacher education curriculum; and students, actual and potential, have an understandable expectation that they will experience a challenging and appropriate preparation for their chosen career.

How are the claims of these various stakeholders to be reconciled? How are national standards of teacher education to be guaranteed? How can we ensure that those who enter teaching are not only well trained but also well educated? How might the existing framework of teaching qualifications be adjusted to take account of changes in schooling? And what is the most appropriate configuration of programmes to ensure that schools recruit the teachers they need, both in number and quality? These are the questions to be considered in the present chapter. The discussion is structured under three heads: national guidelines and competences; the teaching qualification framework; and the pattern of teacher education programmes.

National Guidelines for Initial Teacher Education

All teacher education programmes are governed by national guidelines issued by the Scottish Office. First promulgated in 1983 and subsequently revised in 1993 and again in 1998 (SOEID 1998), the guidelines set out the various requirements which courses must meet. They cover, for example, selection criteria, the major components of the curriculum, the duration of school experience, the phase of education for which the programme provides a qualification to teach, the length of the programme, and the arrangements for partnership between institutions, education authorities and schools. These guidelines are "mandatory": programmes cannot be approved by the Secretary of State unless they comply with the stipulated requirements. When they were first introduced, the guidelines were greeted with suspicion. They were seen as a form of political interference in the work of colleges of education, and as an abridgement of the professional autonomy of teacher educators. There is no doubt that the guidelines did constitute an abridgement of that kind: the question is whether or not it was justified. Arguably, the introduction of guidelines for initial teacher education programmes reflects the increased public accountability within which all educational institutions now must operate. In common with other countries, Scotland has witnessed substantial changes in education in recent years. These changes, for the most part politically driven, have been concerned to enhance the quality of education provided by the schools; to raise levels of achievement; to remove the barriers that impede access to educational opportunities; to confront poverty and social exclusion; to render the educational system more responsive to the needs of industry and commerce; and to achieve greater value for money. It is widely acknowledged that all of these initiatives, intended to improve the educational effectiveness of schools, depend, more than anything, on the quality of the nation's teachers. They are the principal agents of educational change, for it is primarily through their resourcefulness in the classroom that the social transformations expected of the educational system are to be realised. It is, therefore, crucially important to ensure that the education of teachers is in alignment with the new demands that are placed on schools, and national guidelines for initial teacher education are the principal means by which that alignment is to be secured. Through these guidelines a national system of teacher education is established which is integral to a national system of schooling.

However, the guidelines are not to be regarded as authoritarian impositions through which an identical diet is rigidly dispensed to all students on teacher education programmes. The guidelines are the product of consultation and may be said to represent a professional consensus. Besides, compared to their equivalent in England, the Scottish guidelines are not excessively prescriptive. Course developers are not required to emulate Procrustes: they have ample scope for professional discretion and resourcefulness. As a perusal of the various programmes demonstrates, there is significant institutional diversity. Nevertheless, the programmes retain sufficient features in common to have national currency.

Whether or not the reservations expressed about national guidelines were allayed, the revised guidelines of 1993 were seen as a particularly sinister development and provoked considerable opposition. The revised guidelines included a set of "competences" which all teacher education programmes were expected to cultivate and all teacher education students had to demonstrate in order to achieve a teaching qualification. The list of competences, with minor adjustments, was included in the further revision in 1998.

The competences, which appear to derive from a functional analysis of teaching, cover the following areas:

> Competences relating to subject and content of teaching (6)
> Competences relating to the classroom:
>> Communication and approaches to teaching and learning (12)
>> Class organisation and management (6)
>> Assessment (5)
> Competences relating to the school and the education system (9)
> The values, attributes and abilities integral to professionalism (10).

While the 48 competences certainly constitute a formidable list, they have been regarded in places as conferring certain advantages: they are thought to sharpen the focus of teacher education programmes; to provide students with a set of criteria against which they can monitor the development of their professional understanding; to provide tutors and supervising teachers in schools with an agenda for discussion and assessment; and, perhaps above all, to assert that a principal — if not *the* principal — outcome of a teacher education programme is that the graduate is an accomplished practitioner.

However, there are critics — notably Carr (1993) and Humes (1995) — who regard the introduction of a competence-based approach as inimical to the proper education of teachers. They share three concerns. Firstly, the list of competences is thought to offer a heavily reductionist view of teaching as the deployment of "a repertoire of mere behavioural skills and techniques", rather than as a complex moral and evaluative undertaking with strong cognitive and theoretical underpinnings. Secondly, critics argue that the competences concentrate on the *how* of education rather than the *why*. There is a heavy concentration on the techniques teachers are expected to display, with virtually no consideration given to the wider social and educational purposes to which their efforts should be directed. Teachers are therefore cast in the role of technicians: far from seeking to establish a connection between their work and educational aims and values, they are expected to concentrate on the means by which such aims are to be realised. Thirdly, critics find the competence approach "deeply conformist in character". It assumes that there is a consensus on educational practices, failing to acknowledge "the inherent controversiality of educational aims, objectives and methods". The guidelines, it is argued, leave no scope for "students coming to be able to dissent or depart in an imaginative, creative, innovative or critical spirit from the established canons of educational practice". Admittedly, the guidelines document makes reference to the need for students to adopt a critical attitude, but that is interpreted merely as "being accountable to the say-so of others". Carr sums up his criticism in these terms:

> In short, the ideal of the reflective practitioner is also essentially that of the autonomous or extended professional who reserves a basic

right to be critical of current political and social policies and initiatives — rather than that of the restricted professional who routinely carries out other people's instructions irrespective of whether these may be rationally justified as in the best interests of those young people who have been handed over to his professional charge.

Indeed, he maintains that "the pre-competence goal of the autonomous reflective practitioner and that of the post-competence trained executive of guidelines and other instructions pull in quite contrary directions" (Carr, 1993).

How are we to respond to this withering denunciation? A response of some kind is necessary for, as Humes acknowledges, "Those of us working in Scottish TEIs must operate within the framework of the guidelines: not to do so would be irresponsible and would disadvantage our students." Worse than that, since compliance with the guidelines is a condition of political and professional approval, to mount a programme incompatible with the guidelines would be to surrender any involvement in initial teacher education. Moreover, the notion of the reflective practitioner has wide support in the teacher education community. If the competences constitute such a frontal attack on the notion of the reflective practitioner, the outlook is bleak indeed. Must the position be quite so polarised as Carr implies?

In the first place, it is worth acknowledging that the need for explicitness of purpose is now a political as well as a professional imperative. The guidelines and the associated competences need to be seen as the political response to New Right allegations that teacher education institutions (TEIs) were centres of left-wing radicalism, filling students' heads with "barmy" theories and failing to equip them with the skills necessary for the job. It does not matter that that charge was seriously mistaken: if anything, TEIs were frequently criticised for devoting so much attention to the demands of classroom practicalities that they were merely pedalling "tips for teachers": what matters is that the competences were seen as a way of exercising such control over the teacher education curriculum that institutions would be obliged to concentrate more on what were judged to be essential teaching skills. The competences also perform important professional functions. Through them, the General Teaching Council can hold TEIs to account; teacher education tutors and their partner schools have a shared agenda; and students intending to be teachers are left in no doubt about the central preoccupation of their studies. The competences may be said, therefore, to exemplify the kind of transparency now expected of public bodies. More than that, they provide the profession, as well as the wider public, with the assurance that those who qualify as teachers will be competent practitioners.

Secondly, let it be conceded that the competences do not make sufficient provision for the discussion of educational aims and purposes. It is surely a weakness in what amounts to a specification of a teacher education programme not to begin by delineating the social context in which schools will operate and by affirming, however embryonically, the conception of educatedness underpinning teacher education, or the educational aims and values which the competences are intended to cultivate. The impression is created that questions of purpose and intention, of aims and values, are of no concern to teachers: their function is simply to deliver Scotland's version of a national curriculum. That certainly deskills the teacher and deprofessionalises teaching.

Further, while the competences are set out in a relatively neutral way, it has to be acknowledged that competences derive meaning from the context within which they are being deployed. The teacher uses the various techniques and skills listed to achieve certain educational objectives, and the nature of the educational engagement developed by the teacher depends crucially on the purposes that are intended. For instance, the requirement "to apply the principles and practices which underlie good discipline and promote positive behaviour" is open to different interpretations and is context-specific. What constitutes "good discipline" or "positive behaviour" depends crucially on the educational purposes that are being sought at any particular time. The competences, as a whole, then, have to be seen as ways of achieving a range of possible educational objectives, and an effective programme of teacher education is bound to engage students in the analysis of the diversity of educational purposes which schools might pursue. The solution, surely, is not to discard the competences, but rather to ensure that all teacher education students engage in the study of the different purposes of education and of the personal and social aims which the education system promotes. The discussion of the competences on a teacher education programme is bound to require analysis and interpretation, depending on the educational context in which they are expected to be deployed.

Thirdly, the fact that the competence list does not provide a clearer statement of the importance of theoretical studies and of the ways in which these relate to competent professional performance ought not to leave teacher educators without recourse. Clearly, the competence document does not rule out the acquisition of relevant knowledge: the term "professional competence" is assumed "to refer to knowledge, understanding, critical thinking and skills". Accordingly, the competence list makes repeated reference to the language of conceptual understanding: "demonstrate a knowledge of"; "justify"; "evaluate and justify"; and "knowledge of principles". However, it would be pointless to pretend that the competence document offers a balanced account of all of the ingredients of a teacher education programme: the competences predominate. Thus, the 1993 document asserts:

> The government considers that greater prominence than ever before should be given in teacher education to the securing of classroom skills by newly qualified teachers, and that competence in teaching should be the critical factor that institutions must take into account in designing courses. (SOED, 1993)

Again, however, teacher educators should be able to ensure that that imbalance is addressed by developing programmes which engage students in the knowledge base of the various competences: human development, learning and teaching, the social and environmental factors which influence learning, and so on. The aim here is not to provide students with knowledge that somehow or other might be applied in specific educational contexts but, rather, to furnish them with insights and perspectives that can be used to generate the criteria which will provide the basis for the critical scrutiny, modification and improvement of educational practice. In other words, the fact that the competence list may appear to undervalue theoretical studies does not absolve teacher educators from their responsibility to ensure that their graduates bring a sophisticated understanding of relevant theoretical perspectives to their work.

Fourthly, it is necessary to respond to the criticisms that the competences call for "unquestioning conformity to the edicts and instructions of others"; that they promulgate an "essentially conservative view of educational practice"; that they are excessively prescriptive; and that they fail to acknowledge the essentially contested and controversial nature of education. In the first place, it might be rejoinded that the competences may be said to represent a professional consensus: they are widely acknowledged in the teacher education community to offer a credible portrayal of teaching. Indeed, Humes concedes that "many of the items listed are unexceptionable and deal with matters that all teachers would regard as important". The list of competences is a long way from prescribing a single approach to teaching. In this respect, practice north of the border contrasts sharply with what has been described as the "seriously repressive regime" that has been established south of the border. In the view of one commentator:

> The national curriculum for teacher training has made its first appearance. The institutions are told, in exacting detail, what skills and expertise in the teaching of English and Maths primary students are to acquire and the issues and ideas to which they are to be introduced. Teacher training has become painting by numbers, or rather learning to teach by numbers; and, moreover, institutions are to be checked to see whether they are painting carefully and accurately within the lines. (Wilkin, 1999)

In Scotland, by contrast, there has been an attempt to ensure that teacher education is appropriately focused on the skills of teaching without the excessive prescription that has so alienated teacher educators in England.

Indeed, if anything, the Scottish list of competences is perhaps too diffuse, seeking to incorporate what most experienced teachers and teacher educators would recognise as essential features of the teacher's repertoire. The key message communicated is that teaching is an enormously diverse activity, calling for remarkable versatility as well as the mastery of a very extensive range of capacities, probably the most important of which is the capacity to judge which approach applies in any particular context. To claim, therefore, that the competence list is prescriptive is only partly true: it sets out to compile a range of teaching skills and dispositions; it nowhere suggests that there is a single way of proceeding. It is precisely because it is thought to reflect the essential skills of teaching that there is a strong case for requiring teacher education students to demonstrate they have acquired the necessary capacities.

Nor is it fair to maintain that the competences merely delineate narrowly specific skills. Consider the following:

> identify and respond appropriately to pupils with difficulties in, or barriers to, learning and recognise when to seek further advice in relation to their special educational needs;
> respond appropriately to gender, social, cultural, linguistic and religious differences among pupils;
> evaluate and justify the approaches taken to learning and teaching and their impact on pupils.

No knowledgeable person would dispute that these attributes are all integral to the work of a teacher. However, these are all capacities that call for judgement, for knowledge and reflection, rather than specific routinised moves that might be applied in a mechanistic and unthinking way. It is difficult to see how requiring students to acquire these and similar capacities induces a conformist turn of mind or encourages them to adopt a conservative approach to education. These, like others on the list, are demanding qualities. The list may not devote a great deal of emphasis to creativity or imagination or innovativeness. However, the competences under discussion are those to be acquired by the beginning teacher, not the highly proficient or the expert teacher. For all that, the qualities listed call for considerable resourcefulness: there is nothing routine or unthinking or conformist about them.

Arguably, much of the debate that was occasioned by the appearance of the revised guidelines in 1993 is attributable to the use of the term "competence". That, certainly, is the term that is frequently used in occupational training contexts and usually involves endless lists of specific skills with appropriate performance criteria. No doubt the progenitors of the competence list were under pressure, for political reasons, to develop a comparable list for teachers. Either that proved impossible or, as Stronach and his colleagues (Stronach, *et al*, 1994) maintain, the competence initiative became a case of "liberal recapture": the consultation process served to ensure that the list was not professionally offensive. That is why they describe the competences as "a political compromise masquerading as a technical specification". In the compromise no doubt rather too much ground was conceded to the political interest, but at least the resultant list avoids some of the worst features of comparable lists for teachers elsewhere.

Another effect of the political compromise is the ambiguity of the term "competence". That is defined in the *Guidelines* as encompassing "knowledge, understanding, critical thinking and practical skills". Of course, that is expecting a single word to carry too much. As a result, we have a list that is a mixture of skills, dispositions and other qualities. It is probably fair to describe the competences as a list of *desiderata*, capacities that all graduate teachers ought to display. It therefore provides a checklist against which students' achievements or the content of teacher education courses can be evaluated. Viewed in that way, the competences should not be interpreted as defining a whole programme of teacher education or all that is important in the education of teachers. Rather, they represent certain minimal criteria which all courses should meet. Of course, strong and effective programmes might go well beyond the minimum requirements.

If it is felt that these arguments and proposals are not robust enough to counter what is described as the deprofessionalising and illiberal thrust of the competences, there is a further line of defence that might be invoked. Teacher education programmes certainly require the approval of the First Minister; they must also be accredited by the General Teaching Council for Scotland. However, there is a third stakeholder: teacher education programmes that issue in the award of a university must meet the academic requirements imposed by a university senate. The universities are therefore in a strong position to counter whatever illiberal tendencies might be detected by national guidelines and statements of competences. How might universities perform that particular role?

Firstly, universities can insist that programmes meet their own educational criteria: they should comply with university standards of "graduateness". That is, they should cultivate "the general powers of the mind", the capacity for effective communication, for critical thinking, for rational analysis, for independent judgement, and for disciplined enquiry. Secondly, universities can ensure that the subjects that graduates will teach — the various traditions of human reflection and enquiry — are pursued rigorously and in accordance with the general aims of a university education. Thirdly, universities can require teacher education students to engage systematically with those academic studies which underpin professional action: human development and learning; teaching; the impact of family, social environment and neighbourhood on education; and the social and political contexts in which the professional activities of teachers are located. In view of the intimate connection between education and human well-being and the public good, programmes of teacher education located in universities might be expected to engage students in the study of contrasting perspectives on education and its relationship to democracy, social justice, economic and technological change, and the quality of life in the community. And in all these studies teacher education students might be expected to participate in a culture of debate and critical enquiry, and in the discussion of issues that are deeply contested. Set in such a context, the list of competences may be seen for what it is: not a recipe for deskilling teachers, but a forceful reminder that those who graduate as teachers, whatever their other achievements, must be accomplished classroom practitioners.

Teaching Qualifications

Currently, the three types of teaching qualification — the Teaching Qualification (Primary), the Teaching Qualification (Secondary), and the Teaching Qualification (Further Education) — are intended to reflect three separate sectors of the educational system. The Teaching Qualification (Primary) reflects a philosophy of primary education. The central feature of that philosophy is that the teachers' central obligation is to the children in their care rather than to one or other of the domains of human knowledge. The dictum that the primary teacher "teaches children not subjects" asserts that emphasis. Primary education is seen holistically: the various activities which make up the primary curriculum are meant to cohere by being mediated through a single teacher whose responsibility is to nurture the all-round development of pupils. The primary teacher is seen as a generalist, in the sense of having a responsibility for all aspects of the curriculum and for ensuring that pupils undergo a coherent educational experience.

By contrast, the secondary school curriculum has been and remains strongly subject-based. Accordingly, Scottish secondary teachers have been trained as specialists and, over the years, that specialist training has been strongly defended and has even been a source of professional self-congratulation. It has been regarded as the best guarantee that the education of pupils into the major domains of human enquiry and reflection will be undertaken by those who themselves have a secure academic grounding and "who know their subject". Significantly, whereas the Teaching Qualification (Primary) confers an entitlement to teach all subjects in the primary school, the Teaching Qualification (Secondary), as well as the Teaching Qualification (Further Education), confers an entitlement to teach in one or two designated curriculum areas.

Initial teacher education in Scotland, therefore, provides a preparation for one of these three sectors. It is true that some relationship between the sectors has been recognised. For example, a teacher with a TQ (Secondary) may teach in a further education college, although the converse does not apply. Besides, in order to provide much-needed support in specific areas of the primary school curriculum — usually in art, in music, and in physical education — it has been customary for secondary specialists in those fields to support the primary teacher's work in those curricular areas. However, the amount of boundary crossing has been limited, and has certainly not in any way weakened the commitment to sector-specific teaching qualifications. It needs to be questioned whether the traditional pattern of teaching qualifications is well attuned to the changing needs of the educational system. Several developments suggest that alternative arrangements may now be required.

Firstly, the notion of a sharp break between primary education and secondary education has now been discredited. In some European countries the distinction between primary and secondary schooling is not recognised, all pupils undergoing experience of the seven or eight years' basic curriculum covering the 7–14 age range. By contrast, the Scottish arrangements for transfer from primary to secondary education were traditionally marked by serious discontinuities. Secondly, the pedagogy of the primary school, with its emphasis on projects and "activity" methods, gave way in secondary education to more formal approaches, with an emphasis on classroom instruction rather than group work. Where the primary school pupil could expect to have a single teacher, following transfer to secondary education pupils could encounter as many as fifteen or sixteen different teachers in the course of a single week. Finally, there was no structured relationship between the curriculum of the primary school and the secondary school, with obvious dangers of repetition and a failure to build secondary studies on an agreed and established base. Far from a well ordered progression in which pupils moved without loss of educational momentum to the next phase of schooling, transfer to secondary meant that pupils were exposed to such a markedly different educational environment that their progress could be seriously disrupted.

It was to address this and other related difficulties that in 1989 the Scottish Office introduced the 5–14 Development Programme. The title of that initiative asserted the importance of continuity and progression in education and made it plain that the first two years of the secondary school should be less an incursion into new and unrecognised territory than a deeper exploration of familiar fields of study. The national guidelines issued in 1993 emphasised that the aim of the 5–14 Development Programme was "to achieve continuity, coherence and progression in the curriculum". (SOED, 1993) The curriculum structure over the 5–14 age range was seen to consist of five domains of study: language, mathematics, expressive arts, environmental studies, and religious and moral education. They featured throughout the primary school and extended into the first two years of the secondary school. Moreover, the corresponding document setting out the guidelines for the secondary school confirms that "throughout S1 and S2 pupils should engage in learning experiences and activities related to each of the five specified areas". (SCCC, 1999) There is a clear retreat from the notion of the curriculum as a collection of individual subject studies. Indeed, pupils and teachers are urged to see the learning experiences undertaken in S1 and S2 "as a coherent continuation of primary school experiences within the 5–14 programmes of study". Admittedly, there is a subtle "adjustment of title" in the sense that environmental studies becomes "Environmental Studies: Society, Science and Technology", and expressive arts becomes "Expressive Arts and Physical Education". Nevertheless, the five established areas of the primary school curriculum are seen as the framework for planning the curriculum in S1 and S2: "They underline the importance of maintaining momentum, progression, coherence, and continuity throughout the entire 5–14 stage."

The bringing of the S1/S2 curriculum into closer alignment with the curriculum framework operating in the primary school, by encompassing modes of study rather that subjects, offers a way of reducing the total number of teachers involved in a pupil's education and therefore of addressing some of the difficulties that follow from a highly fragmented curriculum. Already, there are discussions in some education authorities suggesting that the low achievements in S1 and S2 are attributable to the extremely disjointed curriculum undergone by pupils. (North Lanarkshire Council, 1999) It is becoming accepted that the full implementation of the 5–14 curriculum into S1 and S2 calls for a less specialised teacher at this stage, one capable of operating more widely than within the specific framework of a single subject. Indeed, the adoption of a common curricular framework linking primary schools and secondary schools suggests that the professional requirements for teaching in the upper primary school and in the early years of the secondary school might be markedly less different than at present, and perhaps may even be identical.

If there is a need to reconsider the requirements of the TQ (Secondary), there is an even stronger case for reviewing the TQ (Primary). Since the latter confers an entitlement to teach across the full age range of the primary school and across the full primary school curriculum, the holders of the TQ (Primary) must be competent to teach from age $2^{1}/_{2}$ to age 12. At the same time, the scope of the curriculum has been extended. New subjects have been added over the years, including Foreign Languages, Education for Sustainable Development, and Information and Communications Technology. In addition, in response to criticisms that established areas of the primary curriculum received insufficient attention, there has been pressure to extend the amount of time devoted to science and technology, to Scottish language and literature, and to literacy and numeracy. As a result of these additions, the TQ (Primary) curriculum requirements cover the following areas of study:

> Language
> Environmental Studies (Social Subjects, Science, Technology,
>   Information Technology, and Health Education)
> Expressive Arts (Art and Design, Music, Drama, Physical Education)
> Religious and Moral Education
> Personal and Social Development.

In addition, "every encouragement is to be given to the students during their course to undertake modern language study".

Those responsible for programmes leading to the TQ (Primary) complain that it now covers so much ground and that the treatment of the curriculum areas is so superficial that its claim to lead to an Honours degree is perhaps open to question. Certainly, the range of issues and concepts set out in the 5–14 guidelines documents require the primary school teacher to demonstrate competence across a very extensive range of studies. Conscious of the need to allow students the opportunity to pursue some studies in reasonable depth, provision has been made in the latest guidelines for students to pursue options or "elements of specialist study". Commendable as that provision is, it merely serves to create even more pressure on an already over-crowded curriculum. For many of those working in teacher education, the TQ (Primary) is now heavily over-loaded, its curricular scope is too wide, and the age range is too great. Indeed, some critics of the system attribute the relatively poor achievements of pupils in primary schools and in S1 and S2 to the inappropriateness of the teaching qualification. Successive reports from HMI reflect this concern. For example, a recent report (SOEID, 1999) reveals that in S1 and S2 attainment was weak overall in 40% of schools; writing was weak in 50% of schools; "problem-solving" in mathematics required serious attention in 65% of schools; and weakness was also detected in environmental studies in 50% of schools. These findings are paralleled by the results of independent researchers, which suggest that achievements of pupils in the primary school are well below expectations and targets. Of course, there are several explanations for these disappointing findings. It is at least possible that one explanation is to be found in the fact that primary teachers do not have a sufficiently strong knowledge base from which to draw because they are required to cover too many separate areas of study in their programme.

There are, therefore, two forces at work which point to the convergence of a teaching qualification to cover the upper stages of the primary school and the first two years of the secondary school: the curricular breadth of the TQ (Primary) might be reduced to allow rather more specialised study; and the excessive specialisation of the TQ (Secondary) might be relaxed to permit greater curricular breadth.

Further pressure on the existing structure has been exerted by the Higher Still Development Programme. The effect of this major national initiative has been to create an integrated curriculum structure and framework of assessment for the post-16 age group. The "cultural divide" that was thought to separate secondary schools from further education colleges has been bridged: further education colleges are able to offer the full range of academic and vocational programmes leading to national awards; secondary school pupils are able to access the academic programmes traditionally offered by schools but can, in addition, undertake study in those subjects that were formerly the preserve of further education institutions. The outcome of this national development is that the distinction between upper secondary education and further education has become blurred; and, in the absence of any real difference between the sectors, at least for pupils in the 16–18 age range, it does not appear to make sense to speak of a TQ (Secondary) and a TQ (Further Education). As has been noted, those with a TQ (Secondary) can teach their subject(s) in further education colleges, and only recently, in January 1999, the Registrar of the General Teaching Council for Scotland wrote to headteachers of secondary schools to intimate that the Council has agreed that those with a TQ (Further Education) may teach in secondary schools, provided that:

    (a) they are employed by further education colleges operating in partnership with the school concerned;

    (b) they hold a teaching qualification;

    (c) they are registered with the General Teaching Council;

    (d) they teach only the subject (or subject areas) in which they hold the Teaching Qualification (Further Education);

    (e) they teach only those following the 16–18 curriculum; and

    (f) they teach subjects not presently offered by schools.

These are seen as "safeguards", intended to ensure that pupils throughout the secondary school are taught by qualified and registered teachers. However, the GTC's recent announcement suggests that there is a need to review the case for maintaining separate teaching qualifications for the secondary school and for further education.

Finally, it must be questioned whether a pronounced specialism in one or two subjects is the most appropriate form of professional qualification to cover all stages of the secondary school. Arguably, the secondary school does not make a sufficiently strong impact on pupils' personal, social and health education. Subject specialists are expected to be able to exploit their subjects in such a way that they can be related to the social realities of young people's experience. In addition, every secondary school offers a programme of Personal and Social Education — taught, incidentally, by teachers who have no formal qualification in that field — which seeks to engage pupils in the study and discussion of choice of lifestyles, personal and social relationships, and other matters of concern to young people. Nevertheless, despite these efforts and despite the impressive work of such bodies as the Health Education Board for Scotland, young people in Scotland have an unenviable record with regard to health, drug abuse, offending, teenage pregnancy, under-age sexual activity, and other indicators of personal and social malfunctioning. Nobody contemplating that evidence dispassionately could conclude that the interventions made currently by teachers, parents, social workers, and others, are proving effective.

Some of these educational interventions are themselves suspect. Specialist teachers have a loyalty to the subject(s) they teach: the whole point of their professional expertise is to engage pupils in activities through which they will come to terms with the intellectual and other demands of the subject. Indeed, from the year 2000, changes are being introduced to the entry requirements for the TQ (Secondary) which will call for an even greater degree of specialisation in teachers and seriously reduce the number of teachers qualifying in two subjects. Moreover, when schools' academic achievements, as judged by national examination results, are matters of public discussion, it is natural that teachers should direct their energies to the academic treatment of their subjects. One direct consequence of this academic emphasis is that the personal and social dimensions of education may receive less attention than they deserve.

The introduction of new community schools — or "full-service" schools — represents an attempt by the Scottish Executive Education Department to grapple with some of these issues. In the words of the First Minister,

New community schools will employ the fundamental principle that the potential of all children can be realised only by addressing their needs in the round — and that this requires an integrated approach by all those involved. (SEED, 1999)

The new community school is a radical intervention and will call for a new and integrated approach to attack problems of under-achievement, multiple disadvantage, poverty and alienation. However, as the new community schools prospectus states, "the principle on which (the new community school) is based is applicable to all schools". Clearly, a rather different kind of teacher will be required if these schools are to flourish and if other secondary schools are to address the difficult social problems currently in evidence in Scotland. The new kind of teacher will require to be capable of inter-professional collaboration and to demonstrate a wider range of skills than the capacity to teach one or two subjects competently.

New Forms of Teaching Qualification

If that analysis of the existing structure of qualifications is valid, what adjustments are required? There are three approaches. The first of these is to claim that the existing structure of awards is appropriate but that the individual awards are capable of modification to take account of changes in the schools. Thus, greater specialist emphasis could be introduced into the upper primary school by providing more opportunities for specialisation within the existing BEd degree framework, as the current guidelines require; by recruiting more PGCE holders to primary teaching, all of whom have academic strengths deriving from their degree studies; and by creating more staff development opportunities so that primary teachers can develop more pronounced expertise in particular areas of the curriculum. In the secondary field, subject specialists might be expected, during their initial training, to broaden their professional base. Currently, for example, those qualifying to teach in science subjects undertake an additional course in "integrated" science, which equips science specialists to teach the science curriculum in the early years of the secondary school. Similar opportunities, it is argued, could be made available for teachers in the social subjects, and perhaps in other domains also. Again, that broadening of the professional base could be a feature of CPD programmes.

A second strategy is to retain the existing structure of qualifications but to introduce a number of other qualifications. One of these, for example, might be intended to develop the kind of expertise that would straddle the upper primary and the lower secondary years. The new teacher would be more of a generalist than a specialist. That is, in addition to training the existing type of specialist in one or two subjects, we might also introduce a qualification in which teachers professed expertise in three or four major areas of the curriculum. For example, it might be specified that two essential areas in the new programme would be in literacy and numeracy. These areas are widely regarded to be the key to subsequent learning and it would strengthen the work of schools if the holders of the new qualification could teach in these areas. If one other curriculum area were required, that might come from social studies, or science and technology, or the creative arts, or personal and social education. Thus, the new "middle years" teacher would bring strengths in literacy and numeracy and one other curricular domain.

There is no doubt that teachers trained in these ways could be deployed alongside existing teachers with a TQ (Primary) or a TQ (Secondary), and could serve equally in the upper reaches of the primary school and/or the lower reaches of the secondary school: they would be capable of exploiting opportunities for multi-disciplinary studies; and they would be well placed to nurture the core skills of communication, problem-solving, and critical thinking that are of such importance for the modern world.

Another new type of teaching qualification might involve those who had academic and professional strength in the social sciences and in health education. Such a programme might include a substantial study of sociology and psychology, and could draw on relevant expertise from medical faculties covering drug abuse, health education, and human sexuality. Such teachers would be able not only to contribute to the teaching of new studies that are demanded by the Higher Still Development Programme, but they could also make a strong contribution to the new community schools, as well as to existing personal and social development programmes. Again, it is emphasised that such teachers would not replace those with established qualifications; they would, nevertheless, significantly enrich the staffing expertise available and help to ensure that the key changes taking place in schools were met by appropriately qualified teachers.

The third strategy is more radical. It involves a restructuring of the teaching qualification framework to accommodate curricular and other changes. It is possible to envisage the provision of teaching qualifications covering *early years* (pre-school to middle primary), *middle years* (covering upper primary and early secondary), and *post-compulsory education* (16 and beyond). While there are attractions in such a scheme it might entail too radical a transformation of teacher education and in the deployment of teachers to win acceptance. Probably a combination of the first and second strategies might be more appropriate, especially if these new forms of teaching qualification were seen as additional to, rather than a replacement for, existing qualifications.

Routes into Teaching

However the qualification framework is structured, there are two principal ways in which programmes of teacher education are patterned: consecutive and concurrent. The first of these involves the completion of a degree programme prior to a one-year programme of professional and educational study; the second involves the concurrent study of a subject with education, involving professional studies and school experience over a four-year period. Both approaches have their defenders. The consecutive approach is justified on the grounds that, since the primary function of a teacher is to engage learners in the pursuit of knowledge and understanding, intending teachers should undertake a sustained programme of academic study in a discipline, in the course of which he/she should acquire that intimate understanding of the structure of a discipline and its distinctive analytical techniques without which the subject cannot be effectively taught. Once that deep familiarity with a discipline and its ways has been acquired, the would-be teacher is in a position to engage in the study of the pedagogical knowledge and clinical experience essential to effective performance as a teacher. A second justification for the consecutive approach is that many students may embark on a programme of higher education without any commitment to teaching as a career and provision needs to be made, if we are to continue to attract people of quality into teaching, for those whose commitment to teaching develops in the course of their higher education, or even after it has been completed and a graduate has experience of other types of employment.

The concurrent approach finds favour with those who maintain that the one-year consecutive route into teaching is altogether too short a time in which to master all the professional knowledge that a teacher needs to be fully effective. He or she may emerge from the programme with a set of basic survival skills, but that is not an ideal form of professional preparation. The preferred approach, therefore, is to ensure that throughout the four years of the undergraduate programme students are able to combine the study of pedagogy and teaching with their developing understanding of an academic discipline. In this way, professional, pedagogical and academic understanding of the subject mature less hurriedly and at a pace which enables the student progressively to come to terms with the demands of teaching. It also enables the academic studies to influence and be influenced by the pedagogical studies.

Research studies which compare these two approaches to education and training for teaching are inconclusive. For example, Draper *et al* (1997), acknowledging the difficulties of making direct comparisons, found "the prevailing view of headteachers" to be that: "PGCE trained teachers are as good but no better than BEd trained teachers". A study of the interim and final reports submitted to the General Teaching Council during the probation period also "showed no difference in the strengths and weaknesses recorded for PGCE and BEd trained teachers". However, a significant number of headteachers — 38% — preferred to employ those who, like themselves, had entered teaching through the BEd route. In a study which analysed the final grades awarded at the end of training, Cameron-Jones and O'Hara (1997) reported that the two courses produced teachers with contrasting strengths: those with a PGCE were relatively stronger on assessment and subject content, whereas BEd students were relatively stronger in the competences relating to classroom communication and management.

Other studies suggest that the consecutive route confers significant advantages. Thus, the Holmes Group (1986), an influential association of the deans of 123 faculties of education in the USA, maintain that education should be discontinued as an undergraduate study altogether. Concerned at the relatively poor quality of students on undergraduate education programmes and at the failure of these programmes to offer an academic programme of sufficient rigour to enable graduates to teach effectively, the Group sees the teaching profession being better served by those who complete a demanding academic programme before undertaking a two-year professional training for teaching. Sir Stewart Sutherland's (1997) study of teacher education and training in England also detected weaknesses in the BEd route: it committed students to teaching at too early a stage, it attracted weaker applicants, and it led to significant wastage. However, since the PGCE "may not, by itself, adequately prepare trainees", he proposed a new pattern of training, one that would consist of two years of undergraduate study, thus providing the student with a stronger academic base than the BEd provided, followed by, in effect, a two-year "consecutive" programme of professional studies and school experience.

The Holmes Group and Sutherland recommendations accord with experience in Scotland, where it is felt that the PGCE, with some seven qualified applicants per place, but a much smaller share of the total intake, is highly selective but, nevertheless, is forced to reject large numbers of potentially very strong teachers. By comparison, the BEd, with about 3.5 applicants per place, usually attracts a much more varied intake. If what was sought was an academically stronger intake into primary teaching, there would be a case for adjusting the balance of intake to allocate a larger share to the PGCE. The Scottish Office target is a distribution of 55:45 in favour of the BEd, but over the years that ratio has been known to vary with, for example, three times as many admitted to the BEd route. That degree of preference for the BEd is well received in teacher education institutions and elsewhere: it is financially more attractive and, in the opinion of many, allows a more thorough preparation for primary teaching.

If anything, the preference in the secondary field is in the opposite direction. Particularly since the incorporation of the former colleges of education within the universities there has been a growth in the number of concurrent courses for secondary teaching, partly to follow the highly regarded model at the University of Stirling, which has provided concurrent programmes since the University was established in 1965, and partly to enable faculties of arts and science to reinforce merger agreements through collaboration with their recently established faculties of education.

Whatever the academic arguments for and against, it is likely that both concurrent and consecutive routes into teaching will be maintained. One argument is that a variety of pathways into teaching is itself valuable. A more telling argument relates to the control of the supply of teachers. It is politically embarrassing to over-produce teachers, for that is to prepare teachers for unemployment. It is even worse, however, to under-produce teachers, for that is to lead to part-time education for some pupils. The existence of the one-year consecutive programme can be used as a regulator, increasing and decreasing the supply in accordance with the projected needs of the schools.

Controlling the supply of teachers has proved practicable as long as there were two standard routes into teaching: the one-year postgraduate route and the BEd in primary, and the one-year postgraduate route and a limited number of concurrent courses in secondary. As flexible patterns of recruitment are introduced through the growth of concurrent and 2+2 structures, control of supply is likely to become more complex and perhaps incapable of being managed at the national level. Currently, an annual exercise is conducted by the Scottish Office in association with the General Teaching Council, the Scottish Higher Education Funding Council, education authorities, and teacher education institutions, to estimate the number of teachers required, taking account of the birth rate, the size of the teaching force, non-completion rates on courses, and other relevant information. Annual intake figures for primary and secondary teaching are then calculated, and it is the responsibility of the SHEFC to distribute the intake among the various TEIs, allocating numbers for PGCE and other routes into teaching. Arguably, a more efficient arrangement would be for TEIs to contract with SHEFC to deliver a specified output of primary and secondary graduates over a number of years, with significant disincentives for non-compliance with the agreed allocations. Apart from enabling the teacher education institutions to plan more sensibly over a longer timescale, the output model would permit institutions to determine themselves what the balance should be between consecutive and concurrent routes. That approach is more attuned to the local decision-making required to accommodate flexibility of provision and the existence of multiple points of entry to and exit from teacher education programmes. It would be for teacher education institutions and their host universities to determine the most appropriate balance between concurrent and consecutive routes, and it is predictable that the universities would be influenced in determining that balance by their assessment of how the quality of recruitment to teaching could be enhanced.

CHAPTER 3

PARTNERSHIP

Introduction

Probably no term is invoked with greater frequency in teacher education than "partnership". It denotes a variety of forms of collaborative activity between teacher education institutions, education authorities, and schools. As will be seen in Chapter 4, new forms of continuing professional development for teachers are creating opportunities for the intensification of collaborative activities and for the emergence of ways of working that fully justify the term partnership. In addition, at least partly in response to the pressures to enhance quality and to demonstrate improvement in standards, education authorities are drawing on the research expertise of the teacher education institutions (TEIs), and of universities more widely, and there are reciprocal benefits in joint initiatives of this kind.

However, in initial teacher education it would be fair to acknowledge that "partnership" has become problematic. It is a mantra under which course planners, teachers and others are made to feel participants in a shared undertaking and come to persuade themselves of the value of their joint activities. Not surprisingly, the meaning of partnership varies with different participants in teacher education, as well as over time. The purpose of this chapter is to trace some of the shifts in interpretation of the meaning of partnership; to analyse two recent attempts to enhance partnership in teacher education in Scotland; and to propose a way out of the present impasse.

The Partnership Principle

The partnership principle derives from acknowledgement of the view that the education of teachers cannot be effectively undertaken by teacher education institutions acting independently. Since the award of a teaching qualification affirms a person's capacity to teach, opportunities require to be created to enable student teachers to become accomplished professionals; to practise the skills of teaching; to engage in the analysis of their own and other people's teaching; to familiarise themselves with the way of life of schools; and, ultimately, to demonstrate that they have acquired the level of professional competence to merit the award of a teaching qualification. Since teacher education inevitably straddles different locations, it is essential that discussions take place with schools to ensure that students are offered a coherent educational programme. In this way, tutors in higher education and teachers in schools become partners: they need to collaborate to ensure that students reach the required standards. The national guidelines for teacher education courses make it an explicit requirement that teacher education institutions and schools operate in partnership of this kind.

The development of appropriate partnership arrangements has encountered difficulties in Scotland, as elsewhere. Indeed, there was a time when, far from seeing themselves as partners, schools and teacher education institutions viewed each other with varying degrees of distrust and even hostility. Teacher education staff were seen as ivory-towered theorists, several removes from the realities of educational life, while schools were frequently criticised for perpetuating "unreflective practice". These mutual antagonisms have given way to more fruitful professional relationships.

There are four principal features of partnership between schools and teacher education institutions, and these reflect changing conceptions of the role and importance of school experience. Firstly, school experience is now regarded as an integral and essential feature of a programme of teacher education. There were times when teaching practice, as it was known, was seen as a kind of interruption to the college course. Indeed, in the old Robbins BEd degree introduced in the mid-60s it found no part in the formal programme and tended to be arranged in ways that caused minimal disruption to the students' academic study. It is now recognised that the central purposes of these academic studies cannot be realised unless they contribute to the process of learning to teach. In an important sense, school experience gives point and purpose to all other parts of the programme, and the national guidelines are right to acknowledge its centrality. The corollary is that higher education staff and teachers in schools must evolve shared understandings of their respective contributions to teacher education.

Secondly, that part of a teacher education programme which was once known as "teaching practice" is now referred to as "school experience" or "placement". That shift in terminology signals the broadening of professional purposes now sought by placing students in schools for extended periods. Certainly, they must continue to observe and practise teaching, and engage in the analysis of their own and others' work in the classroom. However, in addition, students are now required to increase their understanding of those aspects of the work of schools that take place outside the classroom or which impinge on the classroom: schools' pastoral care and guidance arrangements; various forms of support for pupils' learning; child protection procedures; schools' relationships with parents; assessment policies and practices; and the role which the school plays in the life of the community. That is, the practice of teaching forms only a part, albeit a crucially important part, of an induction into the way of life of the school and the varied roles and responsibilities of the teacher.

Thirdly, there has been a transformation in our understanding of the relative contributions of schools and teacher education institutions to the theory and practice of teaching. Formerly, TEIs were thought to provide the theory while schools provided the opportunity for practice. That kind of dichotomising weakened the standing of the school as a training agency, for it implied that its role was primarily to provide a context for applying theoretical perspectives developed elsewhere. It is now acknowledged that theory and practice are developed in both school and TEI. During their university-based studies students have the opportunity to analyse teaching contexts, to practise their capacity to plan, and to rehearse the implementation of teaching strategies. By the same token, when they are in schools students are encouraged by their supervising teacher to reflect on their own and other people's teaching, to consider alternative strategies, and to analyse the causes of success and failure. Insofar as students on placement engage in such activities, they are theorising about teaching; indeed, they are being helped to develop their own theories of teaching as the basis of their practice in the classroom. On that view, as Macintyre (1994) and others argue, placement has a very powerful contribution to make to the development of students' professional and theoretical understanding. The immediacy of contact between supervisor and student facilitates the provision of feedback and the kind of prompting that nurtures the students' capacity for self-criticism and for analysing their own teaching. Theoretical understanding is therefore generated in and through the practice of teaching, rather than by being developed separately and independently of it. In short, it is largely through placement and the skilled interventions of the supervising teacher that the perennial problem of relating theory and practice is overcome.

Fourthly, it is now widely acknowledged that the contributions of schools and TEIs are complementary rather than interchangeable. If they merely duplicated each other's work there clearly would be no need to arrange for teacher education to take place in two separate settings. Wherein, then, lies their complementarity? Teacher educators now differentiate between the theoretical perspectives developed by TEIs in the light of reading and research on the one hand, and the "craft" knowledge of the experienced teacher on the other, the kind of knowledge that may not always be explicit but is based on the cumulative experience of countless interactions with pupils in classrooms. TEIs and teachers, on this view, operate from different knowledge bases. Of course, these two knowledge bases are not in conflict, although the evidence generated by each may on occasions be at variance: rather, each is to be seen as offering a distinctive perspective on teaching and learning. This complementarity of contribution to teacher education is what makes partnership essential.

Whereas in the past it would have been acceptable to secure the involvement of practising teachers in the supervision of students on placement, and perhaps also in their assessment, it is now imperative to engage teachers in all aspects of teacher education — in student selection, in course planning, in course delivery, in student supervision and assessment, and in programme evaluation. That is, partnership is now not only intended to secure collaboration in the management and conduct of placement but, rather, to secure a significant extension of the scope of partnership to involve collaboration on all aspects of initial teacher education. In this way, the scope of partnership is very significantly extended.

Collaborative Partnership

In the contemporary context, then, partnership involves rather more than cross-institutional agreement on the administrative arrangements for teaching practice: it entails a shared understanding of the process of teacher education and of the complementary ways in which schools and TEIs support all aspects of that process. Clearly, even where there is consensus on the interpretation of partnership, the implementation strategies and patterns of institutional relationship may vary, depending mainly on the location and distribution of power between the partners. In that connection, Furlong *et al* (1996) identify a range of partnership models:

1. HEI-based Schemes
2. HEI-led Partnership
3. Collaborative Partnership
4. Separatist Partnership
5. School-centred Initial Teacher Training (SCITT).

The first of these, which is the traditional approach, is now discredited: the university as the dominant partner expects the school to contribute to a predetermined programme. The fifth, in which the school is in control, severely undermines the principle of complementarity by marginalising or discarding entirely the contribution of the university. Models 2 and 4 offer variations in the extent of delegated authority to schools: model 2 operates mainly through trained mentors, who play a central role in the school-based component of the programme; in model 4, the university virtually sub-contracts a substantial part of the programme to a partner. According to Furlong, the HEI-led model is the most widely adopted: it achieves a balance between the authority of the university as the awarding institution and the professional authority of experienced teachers, while maintaining that degree of dialogue and interaction that ought to characterise a relationship between partners.

Based on a separate comparative analysis, Kirk (1996) has identified the principal features of collaborative partnership, the most radical of the models identified by the Furlong study. There are three fundamental ways in which that model differs from the standard and widely accepted approach which Furlong describes as the HEI-led partnership. The first of these concerns *parity*. Traditionally, relationships between HEIs and schools have been asymmetrical: HEIs were expected, as the formal licensing and awarding authority, to "take the lead" or some other euphemism for assuming the dominant role. Collaborative partnership moves beyond established status differences: it involves a sharing of power in a partnership of equals. All aspects of the partnership and the supporting institutional arrangements are therefore the product of negotiation and agreement between the partners. In this respect, university senates might be expected to cede some of their sovereignty in recognition of the professional authority of teachers as represented collectively by the General Teaching Council.

The second feature of collaborative partnership is *reciprocity*. It is often claimed that in standard arrangements partnership is "a one-way process": the school provides a service to the university. In collaborative partnerships both parties enjoy reciprocal benefits. Schools come to view their relationship with a university as a means of maintaining contact with curriculum and other educational developments; teachers are encouraged to adopt a more analytical and critical approach to their own teaching; they are able to exploit the expertise of the university to support staff development in special educational needs, assessment, and a host of other matters; and they can enlist the research strengths of the university in their development planning, in course preparation, in institutional audit, and in the various ways in which, at a time of intensifying accountability, they attempt to evaluate their own educational effectiveness. For their part, universities are able to secure placement opportunities; they can ensure that their research activities are more sharply focused on the work of schools and classrooms and, therefore, are of more direct benefit to teachers; they can enrich and enliven their teaching by illuminating general principles with specific examples drawn from real settings; and through their work with schools they can embed themselves more securely in their local communities. In short, through collaborative partnership the professionalism of teachers is reinforced and strengthened, and the research and teaching activities of HEIs are properly enlivened and authenticated.

Thirdly, collaborative partnership is *multi-faceted*. In its earliest formulations partnership concentrated on arrangements for teaching practice, that part of a programme that was off-campus. Then, by locating school experience in a wider context it came to be concerned with initial teacher education (ITE) as a whole and all of the factors which shape it. Now, in the collaborative partnership ITE itself is embedded in a network of professional relationships covering staff development, research and other forms of collaborative activity.

The advantages of collaborative partnership have been summarised in the following way:

> Collaborative partnership envisaged the universities working in close association with a network of federated schools, sustaining, through joint staff initiatives, co-operative teaching, and academic interchange of various kinds, a culture of professional co-operation and development. Through these various points of contact and joint activity the universities become partners in the revitalisation of the work of the schools and teachers come to enjoy the benefits of engaging in the life and work of the university. (Kirk, 1997)

Collaborative partnership finds its fullest expression in the idea of the *Professional Development School*, which is strongly endorsed by the Holmes Group in the USA and has been introduced in various parts of North America and elsewhere. A professional development school is defined as:

> A school for the development of novice professionals, for continuing development of experienced professionals, and for the research and development of the teaching profession.

Professional Development Schools seek to achieve these objectives in the following ways:

> By promoting much more ambitious conceptions of teaching and learning on the part of prospective teachers and universities and students in schools; by adding to and reorganising the collections of knowledge we have about teaching and learning; by ensuring that enterprising, relevant, responsible research and development is done in schools; by linking experienced teachers' efforts to renew their knowledge and advance their status with efforts to improve their schools and to prepare new teachers; and by creating incentives for (teachers/lecturers) in the public schools and faculties of education and schools to work mutually. (The Holmes Group, 1995)

On this model, then, the university adopts a special relationship with a number of schools, which become a focal point for a wide range of collaborative activities. One of the specific objectives of the professional development school is to enhance not only the learning of teacher education students but also the academic achievements of pupils in the schools. The university commits itself to supporting the school as a learning community, and the professional development school becomes an extension of the work of the university in exactly the same way as the Teaching Hospital.

> The Professional Development School needs to be seen as the major focus for the universities' three-fold mission of preparing teachers…, serving as the research and development arm of the profession, and providing direct services to the schools: just as teaching hospitals assist in the training of physicians, conduct medical research, and provide high quality patient care. (The Holmes Group, 1995)

Numerous advantages flow from this closer and more intensive partnership between universities and schools. It is surely incontestable that both schools and universities benefit from their participation in an undertaking whose ultimate objective is the enhancement of the learning opportunities for pupils and for students. However, even if this more ambitious aim of collaborative partnership is discounted and the central focus of partnership is seen as the effective management of placement arrangements, the advantages of the professional development school are manifest. Firstly, since the partnership extends over several years there is less need for the annual renegotiation of placement opportunities that is such a marked and time-consuming feature of existing arrangements. Significantly, training and staff development are more cost-effective precisely because they are restricted rather than redistributed to new partners on an annual basis. Thirdly, it is easier to maintain close collaboration with a smaller number of schools than a larger number: the wider the network of schools with which a university is associated, the more scattered the geographical coverage, the more practical problems multiply, and the assurance of quality is vitiated by variations and inconsistencies of practice. Over the years, professional development schools can accumulate substantial expertise in the management of students' school-based learning, in supervision and in assessment. And it becomes an especial mark of esteem for them that they enjoy a particularly close association with a neighbouring university.

It is possible to speak, then, of two approaches to partnership: the standard approach which is described by Furlong as "HEI-led" and which is well established south of the border; and the more radical approach which is encapsulated in the professional development school. These correspond to what Kirk (1995) has described as "weak" and "strong" partnership: the first of these incorporates all of the patterns of the standard approach to partnership; strong partnership, on the other hand, has benefits for both schools and HEIs.

> Its principal feature is that collaboration on initial teacher education is not an end in itself but, rather, that collaboration forms part of a web of relationships bringing schools and HEIs into a close working relationship over a number areas of professional work for the mutual benefit of both school and HEI. ITE is one focus for discussion and analysis, but work undertaken in that context reverberates across the whole programme of professional development in the school and the research and development work undertaken by the HEI.

How do Scottish approaches to partnership measure up to these benchmarks? There are two developments to be considered: the Scottish Office teacher mentor scheme of 1992 and the General Teaching Council partnership initiative of 1997.

The Teacher Mentor Scheme

The teacher mentor scheme, like so many other initiatives in Scottish education, was a response to developments south of the border. When in January 1992 Kenneth Clarke intimated that he wished to see a greater part of teacher education located in schools, the Scottish Office became committed to a comparable change. Michael Forsyth, the Minister for Education at the Scottish Office, opted instead for a pilot exercise to test the feasibility in Scotland of allocating a rather larger proportion of time in the PGCE — already standing at 50% — to school-based studies. The letter of 17 February 1992 inviting Moray House Institute of Education to undertake the pilot identified the three essential ingredients "of a more school-based approach to training":

1. a more effective partnership between the college and the schools with selected teachers being more involved in course design and in the training and assessment of students;
2. extension of school-based experience to around two-thirds of the 36-week course;
3. greater emphasis on imparting professional skills.

The "design principles" for the pilot PGCE programme included the following:

rather more than half of the course time should be spent on structured experience in schools;

school experience should be supervised by designated teacher mentors (teachers/ communicators of high quality in collaboration with college staff);

mentors should be involved as equal partners in the assessment of students against defined criteria;

groups of around ten students should be allocated to each base school, preferably in subject pairs;

appropriate training should be provided for nominated mentors.

A highly significant feature of the programme was that additional resources would be available at the rate of £1,500 per student, mainly "to provide replacement of the time of the mentors".

Moray House agreed to undertake the project and in 1992/93 its PGCE (Secondary) contained two groups: the pilot group, consisting of 100 students (about 40% of the cohort); and the non-pilot group. For both groups the aims of the programme and the assessment requirements were identical. However, the pilot group spent twenty-two rather than eighteen weeks in schools; their school-based work was supervised by mentors who had undertaken special training covering student supervision, support and assessment; each mentor worked with two students and a "co-ordinating" mentor carried overall responsibility for the school-based component and for liaison with the TEI.

There were two evaluations of the pilot. The first, built into the design of the programme, was a study by college staff led by the Director of Teacher Education; the second was an independent research study commissioned by the Scottish Office Education Department (SOED) and conducted by the Scottish Council for Research in Education. In reporting their studies both sets of researchers made two important caveats: firstly, despite deliberate attempts by the TEI to minimise it, there may have been a Hawthorne effect in operation: whatever success was recorded might be attributable to the fact that the pilot was the subject of close investigation rather than to features of the pilot itself; secondly, the success of the pilot was perhaps not best measured during or immediately after the end of the programme but, rather, only when graduates have fully established themselves in their careers. Acknowledging both of these qualifications, both research groups drew positive conclusions from the pilot. Cameron-Jones and O'Hara (1993) established that the pilot students were characterised by a higher degree of "school-mindedness" than the non-pilot students: that is, the pilot students attributed their professional development to influences from the school rather than from the TEI or from school/TEI jointly. Other differences in student attitude and achievement, as measured by grades awarded, consistently favoured the pilot group but, in general, the differences were not statistically significant. The same findings were found when the pilot was repeated for a second year in session 1993/94. (Cameron-Jones and O'Hara, 1994)

For their part, Powney and her colleagues (1993) concluded their independent study with these words:

> Increasing the amount of time pilot students spent on school experience, especially with the opportunity to spend a long time in one school, was generally seen as beneficial to the training of PGCE students in the Pilot PGCE at Moray House Institute. Pilot students developed considerable confidence by the end of their course and were comfortable in the school environment.
>
> While putting emphasis on the need for substantial time on school placements, students, their mentors and tutors all agreed that this needed to be balanced by sessions away from school in which they could work with tutors and reflect critically on educational practices and their underlying assumptions.

Clearly, while endorsing the value of extended periods in schools, Powney and her colleagues draw attention to the importance of reserving time for college-based studies. In addition, they repeatedly emphasise the resource implications of the study: the need to protect time for mentors, for the training of mentors, and for adequate additional funding.

In an endeavour to generate wider professional discussion of the issues, SOED arranged a seminar in November 1993 at which Gerald Wilson, Secretary of the Department, appeared to confirm official support for the scheme. He claimed that "both studies of the project confirmed that there were genuine benefits to be gained from the mentor teacher approach: students felt they were better supported; teachers had an enhanced professional role in the teacher training process; and the training institution worked in closer partnership with the schools." He skilfully allayed concerns about the possible shift to a fully school-based scheme by asserting that both schools and training institutions "would continue to have a role in assisting student teachers to develop". But he raised eyebrows when, with reference to the possible long-term development of the scheme, he intimated that "the funding effect should be cost-neutral", strongly implying that no additional funds would be made available and that any difficulties would have to be resolved by redistribution of funds between the partners.

In May 1994 James Douglas-Hamilton, the new Minister for Education, intimated that the teacher mentor scheme, which had been "tested" by the Moray House pilot would be introduced for the PGCE (Secondary) from academic session 1995/96. Since the scheme clearly required "extra dedicated time for teachers involved in training and assessing PGCE (Secondary) students", an extra £2m would be made available over a two-year period "for transmission to schools".

Opposition to the scheme was considerable. For example, in successive years the Educational Institute of Scotland resolved at its annual general meeting "to advise members not to co-operate with proposals which seek to increase school-based components at the expense of college-based components". Faced with such pressure, the Scottish Office exerted maximum pressures on the TEIs to secure the success of the scheme; it decided in July 1995 that the introduction of the scheme would be postponed for one year; and then, bowing to the inevitable, in October 1995 intimated that the scheme would be withdrawn on the grounds that "teacher representatives and education authorities do not believe the time is right for an initiative of this kind when schools are already facing a number of challenges, including the planning and development work for Higher Still".

At first glance it would appear as though the scheme had all the hallmarks of a successful innovation. It recognised the professional entitlement of teachers to participate in training; it acknowledged the commitment of teachers to shaping and supporting the development of future colleagues; it sought to build on successful experience and a pilot study; it recognised that training for mentors was required; and it acknowledged the additional burden it would place on teachers by allocating additional funds to enable staff cover to be provided for mentors.

Why, then, did the initiative require to be withdrawn? There are several explanations. Firstly, there was strong teacher resistance: the mentor scheme was seen as yet another imposition and one, moreover, that was not considered to be central to the work of schools. Secondly, the extension of the school-based at the expense of the university-based studies was thought to be dilutionary. Thirdly, the additional resources allocated were judged to be insufficient. Fourthly, in the TEIs there was a concern that staff were being expected to engage in the training of school staff who would, in due course, assume the responsibilities formerly undertaken by university staff. Finally, it was thought that the scheme was too heavily influenced by developments south of the border and had been introduced out of compliance with UK policy rather than out of a concern to solve a particularly Scottish problem.

The GTC Partnership Initiative

Part of the ministerial U-turn on mentoring was to invite the General Teaching Council in October 1995 to undertake a study of the key elements in partnership arrangements "with a view to introducing a national framework". The GTC accepted that invitation. The working party set up was widely representative of all the relevant stakeholders — the Directorate, Convention of Scottish Local Authorities (COSLA), heads, the teacher education institutions, the Inspectorate, and the Council itself — and was chaired by the Convener of the GTC. It undertook two rounds of consultation, at the start of its work and following the production of an interim report, and consulted also with students in teacher education institutions. The substantial response to the invitation to comment and the positive reception of the report by the GTC itself suggested that the final report reflected a professional consensus in Scotland. Having affirmed the central importance of partnership in initial teacher education, the report identified the two central difficulties. Firstly, there were inconsistencies of practice and degrees of involvement across the country, and, secondly, it drew attention to the under-resourcing of partnership. It maintained that for partnership to be successful "specific allocations in terms of time and resources are essential". The response to these difficulties was two-fold. In the first place, the working party recommended the establishment of a national framework for partnership "to ensure that all students benefit from a consistency of approach". Each teacher education institution was urged, in association with its partner authorities, to establish "a strategic committee which can make broad policy and reach agreements on general practices and procedures". Secondly, while acknowledging that teachers, as professionals, were always "prepared to devote time, much in excess of what is quantified and paid for", it concluded that "additional resources are required to support the professional development needs of school staff, the involvement of school staff in course design and related activities, and in assessment".

It was natural, given the stress that was laid on the provision of additional resources, that the GTC report would be well received by the teacher education community. It was also warmly welcomed by Sir Stewart Sutherland (1997) in his report on teacher education and training for the Dearing Committee. He nevertheless felt that there was a lack of clarity about the meaning of partnership and was emphatic that any national partnership arrangement should "encompass resource issues". His report therefore recommended that the GTC should undertake work "to assess the current costs of partnership and to assess the potential costs under a national framework and to develop proposals for a resource allocation model that guarantees stability and transparency in funding partnership arrangements".

Accordingly, the Scottish Office and the GTC jointly commissioned Deloitte Touche to undertake an analysis of the costs of partnership. The report (Deloitte and Touche 1999a), which was based on full consultation with the six TEIs, with education authorities, with schools, with the Funding Council, and a postal survey of 400 primary and secondary schools, produced some significant findings: only 62% of schools were involved in placement; the costs of placement varied across teacher education institutions; while schools had "a strong sense of duty" towards teacher education, placement imposed extremely heavy demands which tended to erode the teachers' personal time; and the overall costs of partnership were calculated to be between £6.3m and £8.1m per annum. There has been no official reaction to the Deloitte Touche report, although the GTC has committed itself to a national seminar on the topic.

It would be fair to conclude that partnership has been on the agenda in teacher education in Scotland consistently now for at least six years without any sign of permanent resolution. It seems curious that, despite the strong commitment to partnership and, indeed, to collaboration of various kinds, partnership arrangements in Scotland have yet to adopt what has become standard practice south of the border. Further afield, initiatives such as collaborative partnership and the professional development school are operating successfully. What stands in the way of their introduction in Scotland, and why is partnership proving to be such an intractable problem?

There are four obstacles. The first of these concerns the ambivalence in the educational community about any increase in the responsibility of schools in initial teacher education. There is no doubt that many schools are strongly committed to partnership and that they collaborate closely with teacher education institutions. That involvement is taken to be a sign of a school's commitment to the importance of teaching and learning and to enhancing the quality of the teaching profession; it is also a way of demonstrating to parents and others that the school is sufficiently confident in its work to be able to pass on its expertise to new teachers. In a survey of the views of teachers, Stark (1994) reported that "schools and children benefited from (students') presence in the school: student teachers were seen as enthusiastic, willing and (usually) young individuals who brought fresh ideas and specific talents in, say, art and music. Teachers felt that 'having a student' brought them into contact with new ideas and concepts in current thinking in the training institutions. In particular, teachers had an opportunity to stand back and observe their pupils, to reflect on their own teaching, and to evaluate different approaches." More recent studies reinforce that perception. The GTC partnership report saw participation in initial teacher education "as a key feature of (teachers') professional identity". The Deloitte Touche report found "evidence of a strong sense of duty within schools towards teacher education": such was teachers' commitment to supporting the professional preparation of their future colleagues that they allowed student supervision to eat decisively into their "personal time".

Nevertheless, there is evidence of a less encouraging kind. The GTC partnership report found evidence "that there has been in the past some reluctance within the teaching profession to accept a degree of responsibility for its own induction and training". The report believed that members of the educational community, including the teaching profession, "need to be convinced of the value of their involvement in initial teacher education".

Among the reasons given in the Deloitte Touche report for the 38% non-participation in teacher education were the following: teacher education is not seen to be part of the core business of schools; "given the current emphasis on performance assessment" there were "professional risks" involved in diverting attention from improving their own pupils' academic performance; and there is neither recognition nor reward for involvement and no penalty for non-involvement. However, undoubtedly the most inhibiting factor was the impact on the workload of teachers: student supervision was yet another burden that the school was expected to carry. Significantly, Stark (1994) described the involvement of schools in teacher education as "virtually a form of gift-giving". She found evidence that this generosity will not continue indefinitely and that, in the current economic climate, schools and authorities were having to question "for how much longer they can literally afford to go on giving".

There is also ambivalence in the teacher education institutions. As might be expected, these institutions strongly support the centrality of placement in teacher education programmes and accept that effective teacher education depends crucially on the quality of the partnership arrangements. Nevertheless, there is evidence also of a less positive view. Deloitte Touche reported the reduction in the number of placement visits and the less frequent interaction between tutors and school staff. Of course, the direct explanation for any detectable diminution in liaison is attributable to the intensifying resource pressures on the TEIs. Progressive staffing reductions have made it increasingly difficult for TEIs to combine institution-based teaching, research, and consultancy with placement supervision. While there has been no significant reduction in the student numbers, there has been a significant reduction in staffing levels. Since placement tends to be a 1:1 form of teaching, inevitably there has been pressure to reduce the number of visits. Moreover, the amount of staff time spent in travelling to placements, especially when it is not always possible to find schools in the vicinity of a TEI, adds to the pressure. Indeed, schools often have the impression of a harassed tutor moving from school to school, frequently returning to the institution to fulfil a teaching commitment, with the result that, instead of there being time for a full discussion with the student and the supervising teacher, the complex task of maintaining standards is reduced to what is disparaging referred to as "the flying visit".

The second obstacle to the development of partnership is more intractable: it concerns resources. The Scottish Office has maintained over the years that provision is made in the funds allocated to authorities, and therefore to schools, to enable them to participate in student supervision and support for probationer teachers. If that, indeed, is the case, it is surely inequitable that a substantial number of schools play no part in teacher education and suffer no financial consequences for this non-involvement. However, since resources for this function are not specifically earmarked but simply form part of a global sum, schools tend to take a sceptical view and to insist that whatever benefits partnership confers, it also imposes additional costs. In the tightly controlled financial environment in which schools, like other educational institutions, are now required to operate, the expenditure of professional effort requires appropriate resource underpinning, and any extension of responsibility for teacher education in schools is thought to require additional funding. In the purchaser/producer culture that has been fostered by government policy, schools have been encouraged to see themselves as providing a service to the teacher education institutions, who should reimburse them accordingly. In effect, partnership is tending to be seen as much in commercial as in professional terms.

So predominant is the resource problem in Scottish education that every initiative is met with pleas that adequate resources should be made available to secure its proper implementation. The same attitude is encountered in relation to partnership in initial teacher education. There is now a strong professional consensus that additional resources must be found to enable the objectives of partnership to be fully realised. The GTC Partnership Report, the Sutherland Report, and the Deloitte Touche Report all draw attention to the need for adequate resourcing of partnership. The Scottish Office stance implies a redistribution of funds from the TEIs to the schools, bringing practice north of the border into line with the position in England, where transfer of funds is standard practice. However, if the TEIs were obliged to fund partnership by transferring funds to schools at the going rate of roughly £1,000 per student per year, the financial viability of most of the TEIs would be at risk.

Not surprisingly, in order to avoid any possible financial embarrassment, the teacher education institutions have sought to emphasise the professional advantages of partnership, re-asserting the responsibility of the profession in initial teacher education, and reminding partners of the educational and other benefits that flow to schools through participation in partnership activities. This vulnerability of the teacher education institutions makes them extremely hesitant about recommending the changes that are required to protect and enhance standards in initial teacher education. Consequently, with the exception of the University of Stirling, which has a well established and funded partnership system in place, Scottish teacher education institutions find themselves at an impasse: they are aware that the existing arrangements are open to serious criticism; and they acknowledge the need for reform. However, they are also aware that any significant shift from the *status quo*, especially if it entailed additional responsibilities for schools — as it assuredly would — must expose their vulnerability, for it would lead to a call for additional resources which are unlikely to be found except at their expense.

The third obstacle to partnership development is that in Scotland there is a widespread opposition to the notion of special training schools. Repeatedly, discussions at the General Teaching Council and elsewhere point to the desirability of a dispersed model of training. That is thought to spread more equitably the burden imposed by placement supervision and to create more placement opportunities. It also enables a wider range of teachers to participate in teacher education. However, the basic opposition to concentrating training in a limited number schools rests on a rejection of the notion of training schools or "centres of excellence". These are thought to be alien in a country "which perceives the teaching tradition as one of equality, autonomy, privacy, and professional relationships among teachers that are essentially egalitarian". (Brown, 1996) Of course, as has been noted, there are significant educational and financial advantages in concentrating initial teacher education in a more restricted number of schools: since students are inevitably grouped in larger numbers, they can provide support for each other; and the larger grouping justifies the investment in the preparation of a student induction programme, which can make heavy demands on the time of senior members of the staff of schools. Even the GTC report on partnership (GTC, 1997) agreed that the concentration of training in a smaller number of schools conferred "consequential benefits" in terms of the deployment of resources.

Finally, perhaps the central difficulty in the further enhancement of partnership arrangements in Scotland is that, while participation in student supervision is part of the contract of employment of teachers in the sense that they are required "to contribute to the professional development of colleagues, including probationary and student teachers", participation in teacher education is still a voluntary activity: TEIs cannot compel schools to participate. As Humes (1995) has argued, it was precisely the powerlessness of teacher education institutions to require schools to participate in student supervision that led to the collapse of the teacher mentor scheme. Clearly, as long as that position remains unaltered, and as long as these obstacles remain, any enhancement in partnership arrangements in Scotland, at least in ITE, is likely to prove an uphill struggle.

A Way Forward

In the face of these difficulties, what lines of action might be contemplated in the interests of enhancing partnership arrangements? There is a pressing need for action, if only because the new arrangements being introduced by the Quality Assurance Agency for Higher Education will require that as much attention is devoted to the quality assurance of off-campus learning as is currently devoted to university-based studies. Institutions will be under pressure to demonstrate that their placement arrangements rest on more solid foundations than the present voluntary arrangement, in which it is virtually impossible to insist on demanding quality assurance arrangements. What measures, then, might be adopted?

In the first place, TEIs in discussion with schools might continue the discernible move towards the involvement of a smaller number of partner schools at any one time. For reasons given above, it would be important to establish that there was no intention to create a limited number of training schools: it would need to be argued that, for quality assurance reasons, and in order to maximise the investment in training as well as to secure the educational advantages that occur when students undertake placement in larger groups, it had become necessary to restrict the number of schools involved.

Secondly, it would be essential for universities to make the resources available, including the costs of cover, if necessary, to ensure that all teachers involved in student supervision were trained for that purpose. There is no doubt that the quality of the supervision and the robustness of the assessments made will depend on the provision of training of that kind. Indeed, there is a case, as in some other professions, for identifying accredited tutors. This difficulty might be resolved for teacher education institutions if the McCrone Committee of Inquiry supports the establishment of the expert teacher, which will form part of the framework of continuing professional development for teachers. Clearly, one of the functions of such expert teachers could be to engage in student supervision, for there would be something perverse about not ensuring that student teachers were exposed to the profession's most accomplished practitioners.

Thirdly, universities might continue to develop the role of the *link tutor*, the member of staff who is associated with a particular group of schools and comes to know them well and to be known by them. That tutor is the bridge linking the resources of the university with the school. In return, the link tutor is able to plan with the regent or another senior member of school staff a programme of activities intended to engage students in the analysis and exploration of whole-school issues such as support for learning, the school's arrangements for pastoral care, discipline, and other matters.

Fourthly, the new developments that are currently under discussion on the revised arrangements for quality assurance in initial teacher education offer scope for the enhancement of partnership. The new arrangements, of which the central feature will be the "collaborative review", are intended to bring TEIs, HMI, GTC, schools and authorities into a much closer working relationship. There are two necessary developments: on the one hand, the GTC might become much more assertive in specifying the criteria that should govern TEI-school partnerships and the conditions which schools must meet for participation in initial teacher education; on the other, HMI might press to ensure that, in developing the instrument that plays such a key role in school self-evaluation, there were performance indicators covering student supervision and support. If these two suggestions were incorporated into the revised arrangements, partnership would be significantly strengthened, as would the quality of teacher education in Scotland.

Finally, and perhaps more radically, there is a need, even within the resource constraints presently imposed, for a switch in the role of the visiting tutor. If a more restricted number of schools is involved, and if appropriate training is provided, supervising teachers can reasonably be expected to provide more valid and reliable assessments of students' work. The role of the visiting tutor, as assessor, would therefore lapse. It would still be necessary to ensure that there was appropriate moderation in the grades awarded by supervising teachers in different schools, and that moderating function could be combined with other quality assurance functions undertaken by the visiting tutor as a representative of the university as awarding body. A development of that kind would certainly strengthen the existing arrangements; it would fully recognise the distinctive perspective of the supervising teacher in the assessment of students' work, and would allow more confidence to be placed in judgements made by those who had been trained for the purpose.

It would be a necessary feature of these revised arrangements that the university would go out of its way to ensure that supervising teachers, if they did not have a special designation, such as the "teacher fellow" used by the University of Stirling, would be recognised in other ways. It would be important to do so to emphasise the important role played by practising teachers in maintaining the standards of the university, as well as of the profession.

CHAPTER 4

THE PROFESSIONAL DEVELOPMENT OF TEACHERS

Introduction

No-one now believes that the quality of the teaching profession, as judged by its capacity to make a decisive impact on pupils' scholastic achievements, is to be secured simply by ensuring the highest standards of initial teacher education. However comprehensive or thorough that initial preparation may be, it cannot equip teachers with all the skills and understandings they will require throughout their careers. The school curriculum is not a static entity: new subjects are introduced; established knowledge in familiar disciplines is quickly eroded; new approaches to learning and teaching are recommended, some of which are admittedly merely passing fads, but there are others which become essential features of the effective teacher's professional repertoire; and new objectives for the educational service are set, frequently reflecting changing political priorities, which can require radical departures from teachers' established ways. Inevitably, therefore, as public, parental and political expectations of the school system are raised, so the pressures for schools and teachers to change intensify, for it is now acknowledged that the aims of curriculum renewal and reform are unrealisable without modifications to teachers' practices. In the words of the late Lawrence Stenhouse, there is no curriculum development without teacher development.

However, the professional development of teachers is not to be seen simply as a response to changes in the curriculum, or the circumstances of schooling, or any other kind of external pressure. Teaching is a professional activity: it implies a commitment to enhanced performance; and it entails a continuing search for more sensitive and intelligent ways of enriching pupils' educational experience. So complex are the demands of teaching, indeed, that no teacher worthy of the designation would ever claim to have achieved such mastery of the craft that there was nothing more to do or learn, or that further improvement was impossible. Indeed, perhaps *the* hallmark of the professional teacher is that he or she holds open the possibility of enhanced performance, not as a response to political diktat, not as a form of compliance, not in fulfilment of a contractual requirement, but as the expression of an inner professional commitment to improved practice.

Whether the professional development of teachers is seen as the means of transforming educational provision or as rooted in the impulse to improved performance, all teachers should have opportunities to engage in relevant professional development activities which articulate with initial teacher education and extend throughout their careers. In his analysis of the current scene in Scotland, Marker concludes as follows:

> The key lies in career-long professional development of a high quality, but, in practice, professional development has been one of the poor relations of the education service. Teachers have not been willing to campaign for it at the expense of salaries or class sizes; the authorities have regularly had to sacrifice it to meet their statutory responsibilities; successive governments have advocated it without providing the necessary resources, inhibited by the costs of doing so for a labour-intensive profession whose clients require constant supervision. Unless the situation changes, professional development for many teachers will continue to be an *ad hoc*, low-level activity, whose value they are sceptical of and which compares ill with that demanded by other professions. (Marker, 1999)

The purpose of this chapter is to offer an alternative to Marker's somewhat gloomy interpretation, in the light of recent developments.

Current Provision

As Marker acknowledges, responsibility for continuing professional development (CPD) in Scotland, as elsewhere, is located at three levels: the individual school, the education authority, and, exercising national responsibility, the Scottish Executive Education Department (SEED). That distribution of responsibility is manifestly appropriate. The school is a natural unit for CPD activities: staff exercise front-line responsibility for the quality of the educational experience the school promotes; they are well placed to identify, in the light of their own evaluation of the school's educational effectiveness, where their CPD needs lie; and it is in the school setting that alternative approaches to teaching and learning are to be tested. No doubt schools find it difficult to protect sufficient time for CPD and may find it convenient to allow planned activity time to be deflected to activities that have more to do with maintaining the bureaucracy of the school rather than its educational resourcefulness. Nevertheless, there are considerable attractions, surely, in an educational system in which each school, as a centre of learning, affords appropriate priority to fostering the professional learning of its teachers.

Even if schools were able to establish themselves in this way, there would be a need for CPD on a broader scale. As individual units, schools are possibly too small for the effective planning of a comprehensive programme of CPD activities. Education authorities have a wider strategic responsibility and they have considerable experience of providing CPD opportunities that either centre on clusters of schools or are extended to specific categories of teacher on an authority-wide basis. As employers, authorities have an obligation to promote the professional well-being of teachers and to provide them with the support that is necessary if they are to offer an effective service. It is reasonable, therefore, for authorities, through their advisory or some other support service, and through secondments of appropriately experienced and knowledgeable staff, to complement the CPD provision provided by individual schools.

Finally, education authorities operate within a national system of education and are expected to comply with national priorities in education as in other spheres. Since curriculum development and other forms of educational change have in recent years been politically driven and energetically pursued from the centre, authorities have increasingly been seen as responsible for the implementation of national initiatives and plans. Each national educational initiative has CPD implications and, over the years, priorities for CPD have been identified annually, deriving directly from national developments. The fact that difficulties have been encountered in the implementation of practically every national development — from Standard Grade in the early '80s to the current preoccupation with Higher Still — does not invalidate the need for national staff development strategies, reflecting the priorities with which authorities are expected to comply. A key task at both school and education authority levels is to interpret local CPD needs against priorities that are determined nationally, albeit on the basis of consultation with authorities and other stakeholders.

One of the principal advantages of the current CPD arrangements in Scotland is that needs are identified by the educational system itself — by schools, by authorities, and by SEED — rather than by the providers of CPD programmes. As Marker has noted, traditional CPD provision was TEI-based rather than school-based: teachers attended courses and were expected to return to their schools imbued with fresh ideas and novel ways of working which could be shared with colleagues. That approach to CPD provision has been discredited: it was thought to allow providers to determine the CPD agenda; it offered training that was frequently decontextualised and did not take account of the particular circumstances of schools; and it was thought to encourage a degree of dependency that inhibited teachers from actively seeking solutions to their own professional problems. Whether or not these criticisms were justified, there was widespread support — if not in the TEIs themselves — for the switching of resources from the TEIs to authorities and schools, thus allowing the so-called "users" to control CPD provision.

Of course, the TEIs continue to offer programmes based on their assessment of the professional needs of schools and usually following consultation with neighbouring authorities. They have long maintained that, while there are advantages in school-based in-service education and training (INSET) and CPD, there are also significant benefits to be derived from attendance at courses: teachers can encounter fresh ideas and approaches, often the fruits of research and development work; they can experience dialogue with teachers from other schools and settings; and they can be encouraged to adopt a less inward-looking and parochial approach to educational provision. Consequently, while most CPD provision is now school-based and education authority-based, a significant amount of this provision is led by staff in the TEIs. In addition, substantial cohorts of teachers, at their own expense and in their own time, are enrolling on CPD programmes at TEIs. Undoubtedly, one of the attractions of current provision is that it is part-time, modular, and based on the credit accumulation and transfer principle. Partly funded by SHEFC, a national system of awards has been adopted by all TEIs with the 30-hour module as the basic unit of academic currency. The completion of four modules leads to the award of the postgraduate certificate; eight modules leads to the postgraduate diploma; and the subsequent completion of a major dissertation, also equivalent to four modules, leads to the award of the Master's degree. While it is common for such schemes to be based on pathways — for example, in special educational needs, in management, in guidance and counselling, in curriculum, pedagogy and assessment — most allow very considerable flexibility with regard to choice and the pacing of studies. Scotland, therefore, has a national structure of awards which is an appropriate mechanism for recognising achievement in CPD.

Much CPD provision that is school or authority-based will be less sustained than the 30-hour module. In order to maximise participation in CPD all TEIs offer substantial opportunities for the accreditation of prior learning. Thus, a teacher who has undertaken a programme of development activity within a school, or who has attended one or more authority-based INSET courses, can apply to have such activities accredited as part of a pathway leading to an award. In this way, school-based INSET, work that is clearly related to the professional development needs of teachers in a particular school, achieves the same kind of recognition as attendance at a TEI-based programme and teachers thus have an incentive to pursue their own professional development.

The Sutherland Report

Sir Stewart Sutherland's review of teacher education and training, conducted as part of the Dearing/Garrick Committee of Inquiry into Higher Education, naturally included an analysis of the CPD of teachers. (Sutherland, 1997) While Sir Stewart reported that "the evidence presented to me with regard to CPD suggests that its importance in strengthening the professional role of teachers is more widely recognised within Scotland", there was a need for three changes. In the first place, as Draper *et al* (1997) had shown, arrangements for probation and induction of teachers appeared haphazard and inconsistent: there was a need "for a coherent induction programme for teachers that builds on the period of initial training". Secondly, while the current variety and diversity of courses was "commendable", there was a case for ensuring that it was "structured within a national framework in which all provision is accredited and in which there is agreement on the range and level of CPD that should be undertaken by teachers at different stages of their careers". Finally, the report drew attention to weaknesses in the funding of CPD. What was required was "a system of funding CPD that is both transparent and stable, and which ensures a degree of consistency across the country". Significantly, the GTC was seen as playing the lead role, in consultation with others, in addressing all three of these recommendations.

The Scottish Office responded to the Sutherland Report recommendations in February 1998. Reflecting the consensus which supported the Sutherland Report recommendations, ministers "invited the GTC to build on its work in (probation) by undertaking an analysis of the effectiveness of the current arrangements and considering the practicalities and implications of developing a coherent induction programme for teachers". In response to the recommendation on a national framework, the Department intimated that its development proposals would be set out in a forthcoming consultation paper.

National Consultation Paper on a Framework for CPD for the Teaching Profession in Scotland

The consultation paper duly appeared in July 1998. It began by acknowledging the shortcomings in the existing arrangements: "beyond initial teacher education there are no statements of additional competences as standards to inform development, no overall framework to give coherence to teachers' development, and no structure of qualifications to work towards that gives recognition to teachers' increased remits and professional skills". Moreover, there was "no general obligation on teachers to undertake professional development or training leading to further qualifications" and "no financial recognition by employers, or formal recognition by the GTC, for those who achieve additional qualifications; nor is there any change in job title or description to reflect the additional qualifications". The consultation paper argued that these shortcomings would be remedied "if development and training were to be underpinned by a formal structure of competences and standards which was clearly stated and made widely available".

The national framework proposed would consist of a hierarchy of *standards*. Each standard would be a benchmark of professional achievement and a milestone of career progression; each would be accompanied by an elaborated set of competences, the achievement of which would testify that the necessary standard had been attained. Where appropriate, each standard would relate directly to a postgraduate award, in this way bringing professional standards and academic awards into an integrated framework. Finally, teachers would be supported in reaching each standard by completing its associated programme of professional development activities and studies. The establishment of such a national system of linked and progressively more demanding standards was thought to confer several benefits: it would enhance the quality of teaching and learning; it would give teachers greater job satisfaction; it would serve as a guide for teachers in their career planning and development; and it would ensure that whatever training was provided was sharply focused on the professional competences relating to one or other of the standards of the framework.

It was imperative that the new standards should align with the standard and associated competences already well established for initial teacher education. Beyond that, the following standards were proposed:

(a) "a statement of the standards teachers much reach by the end of the period of probation in order to grant full registration by the GTC". This standard would clarify the requirements to be fully registered as a teacher in Scotland. In addition, the existence of the standard would lead to a greater degree of consistency and transparency about the level of achievement marked by final registration and would therefore provide a more secure base for subsequent professional development.

(b) "a statement of the standards for very good teachers who wish to develop their careers in the classroom". This second standard would relate to "the performance levels of very good classroom teachers … who see career development in the classroom as an important end in itself and have no wish to see themselves promoted out of the classroom". It was considered that the standard would include such matters as teaching consistently to a very high standard; motivating pupils and creating a culture of achievement; striving for constant improvement in teaching and the learning of all pupils; knowing about, practising, evaluating and reflecting critically upon methods of teaching; and reading widely and keeping up-to-date with developments in the subject.

(c) "the standard for teachers who wish to develop their careers in, for example, pastoral care/guidance, or in supporting pupils with special educational needs, or in leading and managing an aspect of the school or an area of the curriculum". Since these roles called for new skills and competences it was reasonable to expect those who aspired to perform them to have demonstrated that the necessary competences had been acquired.

(d) "the standard for teachers who wish to undertake leadership and management responsibilities mainly outwith the classroom at senior management level". The government had already demonstrated its commitment to the idea of a national framework by disclosing that work had already been initiated on the development of the key feature of the framework, the Scottish Qualification for Headship (SQH), which had been taken forward in line with a manifesto commitment "to establish proper qualifications and training for the post of headteacher".

Reporting on the response to the consultation paper in December 1998, the Scottish Office concluded that "the responses received are sufficiently encouraging for the Department to proceed towards the development of a national framework of CPD".

Scottish Qualification for Headship (SQH)

Even before it had initiated the consultation process on the development of a national framework for CPD, the Scottish Office had embarked on the establishment of the SQH. The Labour Party's policy document, *"Building Scotland's Future — Labour's Compact for Scottish Education"* of February 1997, declared:

> Labour will boost the leadership and management skills of headteachers with a new Scottish qualification for all teachers who aspire to become heads.

Soon after taking office, it issued a consultation paper *Scottish Qualification for Headteachers* setting out proposals for a new award. The consultation showed that "in general there was an acceptance that appropriate standards for prospective headteachers and associated development opportunities should be created". The new Standard and its associated competences were set out in *The Scottish Qualification for Headship* (1998). The starting point in the elaboration of the Standard was the adoption of "the key purpose of headship":

> To provide the leadership and management which enables the school to give every pupil high quality education and which promotes the highest possible standards of achievement.

The achievement of that key purpose was taken to involve a set of *professional values* ("commitment to educational values"; "commitment to their own learning in continuous professional development"; and "the capacity to demonstrate their knowledge and understanding"); four *key management functions* ("managing learning and teaching"; "managing people"; "managing policy and planning"; and "managing resources and finance"). From these four key functions there were derived ten *core activities*, such as establishing systems for the delivery of effective learning and teaching; recruiting and selecting teaching and support staff; securing and allocating resources to support effective learning and teaching; and monitoring and controlling the use of resources. Finally, the standard identified *professional abilities* which were sub-divided as "interpersonal abilities" and "intellectual abilities". In this way, the standard seeks to specify "the key purposes of headship and the professional values, management functions, and professional abilities which describe competence in headship". (SOEID, 1998) It constitutes "the standard" against which those aspiring to be headteachers are to be assessed in order to determine their development needs and professional capabilities.

The programme devised to develop the standard of headship consists of four units. Unit 1, "The Standard for Headship in Scotland", is university-based, extending for 2–3 months; Unit 2, "Managing Core Operations", is school-based and extends over 9–12 months; Unit 3, "Managing School Improvement", is also school-based and is of similar duration; while Unit 4, "School Leadership", is institution-based and extends over 3–4 months and includes a brief placement in a non-educational context. For a highly experienced head, an accelerated route has been proposed in which candidates (the term used to define a course member of the SQH programme) undertake an abbreviated form of Unit 1, but must demonstrate competence in all four management functions before proceeding to Unit 4 and the final assessment. (SOEID, 1998)

There are several features of the standard and associated programme that are particularly noteworthy. Firstly, the standard for headship as articulated is academically and professionally defensible: it is an authentic portrayal of an exposed, complex and demanding role upon which a range of accountabilities — for enhancement of quality, for improvement of standards, for greater value for money, for the well-being of staff and pupils — exert themselves with intensifying pressure. The effective performance of that role certainly requires the capacity for judgement that comes from long experience of exercising responsibility in an educational setting and for those modes of working that are learned from observation and from practice. However, that form of experiential learning is no longer sufficient: the complexity of the demands of headship now require systematic engagement in relevant theoretical studies. These studies offer frameworks for the analysis of the tasks of management and leadership; they offer criteria for the evaluation of the performance of managerial skills and practices; and they equip headteachers with the tools necessary to undertake that more rigorous analysis of self, of the school, and of its wider community and political context which headship now requires. The SQH acknowledges that quantum shift in the demands of headship which makes the completion of a programme of postgraduate study a prerequisite for undertaking the role. Secondly, the SQH attaches high value to work-based learning. Two of the units involve the completion of sustained school-based projects, which are supported by study guides and three other forms of support — from the school mentor, from the education authority, and from the university.

Work-based learning is based on two assumptions. Firstly, in professional programmes theoretical studies should be applied to the solution of real tasks undertaken by the candidate as part of the school's development planning cycle, the monitoring of its mode of operation, and the development of measures through which the school's educational effectiveness will be enhanced. To guard against the possibility that theoretical studies remain dormant or inert, merely a form of intellectual embellishment, studies need to be used to effect a difference in the candidate's professional circumstances. In that sense, work-based learning is a mode of technology transfer in professional settings. Secondly, work-based learning, by requiring candidates to relate theoretical study directly to their on-going professional activities, enables them to internalise a personal philosophy of headship and to acquire the capacity to problematise professional experience, to treat theoretical perspectives as hypotheses to be tested in action, so that the disposition to analyse and reflect becomes an essential feature of professional life. To the extent that candidates come to see themselves as researchers in their own institutions, they are analogous to other postgraduate students whose programme entails a significant research component. Certainly, a common requirement of the SQH candidate and other postgraduate students will be the submission of substantial projects which demonstrate academic achievement and which are analysable and assessable in a public way, in relation to the standards of a postgraduate award. At the same time, they entail the completion of essential school-based development tasks.

The third feature of the SQH is that it requires universities and education authorities to collaborate closely in the planning, delivery, assessment and development of the programme. Partnership of that kind is familiar in initial teacher education and in other areas of the work of universities. In these initiatives it is now accepted that professional education entails the integration of complementary perspectives: the experience and insights of the experienced practitioner on the one hand and the theoretical understanding based on research provided by the university lecturer on the other. However, this principle of complementarity has never been so explicitly endorsed in a programme of advanced professional education as the SQH requires. The university tutor and the associate tutor from the education authority will require to collaborate closely in supporting the candidate's studies and professional development activities. By requiring the university tutor and education authority staff to work together in this way, the new award will be a catalyst for enhanced collaboration between the university and its partner authorities.

Finally, the SQH calls for the exposure of candidates to perspectives from the world of business, commerce and industry. Schools are under increasing pressure to take account of commercial principles and there is value in a programme of advanced professional education for heads which enables them to engage with those whose primary leadership function is commercial or industrial, rather than educational. The justification for this requirement is to encourage candidates to come to a richer understanding of the demands of leadership by studying it at first hand in a comparative setting.

If the SQH represents a significant advance in CPD provision, the strategy by which it was developed was no less noteworthy. The SQH originated in the Scottish Office-funded research and development activities of a team of management training specialists, whose work issued in a report, *A Framework for Leadership and Management Development in Scottish Schools* (Casteel, *et al*, 1997). That report provided the basis for a subsequent consultation paper on the features of a new award for heads. Two of the specialists who had produced the framework document, Casteel and Reeves, were subsequently commissioned by the Scottish Office to develop the standard for the SQH. A National Development Unit was established; a National Advisory Committee was appointed; and a cycle of consultation was undertaken to test the acceptability of the proposals and to ensure that these were in line with the expectations of authorities, of headteachers, and of higher education institutions. In keeping with the research and development orientation of the project, the first two cohorts took the form of a pilot and extended pilot, and a formative evaluation study was undertaken to ensure that adjustments to the programme were well grounded before it was more widely distributed across HEIs in Scotland.

Of course, centre-periphery models of curriculum development have well known dangers and the Development Unit sought to avoid these by extensive consultation; by insisting that tutors from authorities and HEIs undertook appropriate training; and by developing materials to support the work of both tutors and candidates. While the Development Unit played a key leadership role in the establishment of the standard and in the conduct of the first two cohorts, by involving tutors from authorities and HEIs across Scotland, they paved the way for its dispersal to and adoption by HEIs in different parts of the country. The national character of the initiative was emphasised by inviting HEIs to tender for recognition as "approved providers", in the full knowledge that they were seeking to participate in the delivery of a national programme, albeit one that had been approved by universities separately, to be delivered in accordance with national quality assurance standards.

Significantly, the SQH attracted additional resources. The response to the consultation paper demonstrated that the new award "would require adequate additional and dedicated funding to ensure quality and access". It was an initiative that was central to the government's drive to raise standards in schools and was therefore one of nine programmes supported by the government's Excellence Fund. Having received funds from central government, education authorities were then in the position of purchasers, and in the bidding system that was established HEIs were obliged in fixing charges to have regard to the discipline of the market-place.

The Completion of the CPD Framework

The SQH was established as the apex of the national CPD framework. Since the standard of initial training had already been marked by the initial teacher education competences, it was necessary to complete the intervening standards. The GTC has been commissioned to establish the standard for probation, the level of achievement marked by final registration as a teacher in Scotland. In November 1999 the Minister, Sam Galbraith, reinforced SEED's commitment to the creation of a national framework. He declared the government's commitment "to strengthening the skills, subject knowledge, and professionalism of teachers throughout their careers" and insisted that professional development "should be the expectation — and entitlement — of every member of the profession". Subsequently, institutions were invited to tender to undertake the development of the standard for "the expert teacher". That standard is expected to include a set of generic competences, "coupled to a set of electives for specific capabilities, for example, in special educational needs, guidance, and other fields". In this way, the government has decided to bring the standard for the expert teacher and the standard for specialist roles into close alignment, rather than as separate stages in teachers' career development. Another significant change is that the government envisages a standard beyond the SQH, with the result that those tendering for the contract will be expected to develop appropriate provision for the highly experienced headteacher.

The strategy adopted by the GTC in the development of the probation standard and the wording of the specification for the expert teacher standard both make it clear that the SQH is the model for the development process. On that model, the development work will involve extensive consultation with the educational community; the specification of the competences which will constitute the standard; the development of a programme of activities which will lead to the achievement of the standard; and the association of the standard with a postgraduate award of a university.

The fact that the various standards in the national framework will issue in university awards is significant. As was noted in Chapter 1, universities now carry a major responsibility for initial teacher education. The development of the national framework for CPD therefore gives the universities an unprecedented opportunity to influence the character and formation of the teaching profession in Scotland. Of course, that influence is circumscribed: initial teacher education has also to be formally accredited by the General Teaching Council, and the awards of the national framework have to meet criteria which place a strong emphasis on professional competence and performance. If teacher education and teachers' professional development were formerly marginalised and did not receive the attention their importance deserved, the location of all of these studies within a university setting leading to university awards may be seen as a significant step in the further professionalisation of teaching.

The development work for the standard for the "expert" teacher and related roles is expected to take two to three years. Within that period, therefore, Scotland will have a systematic framework for CPD with clearly defined standards and associated competences leading to postgraduate awards. While the establishment of that framework will raise the profile of CPD and perhaps encourage stronger participation by teachers, it will not by itself secure the level of participation that is essential if the standard of teaching is to be enhanced throughout the country. How is that objective to be secured?

Firstly, it might be stipulated that career progression as a teacher will be conditional on the achievement of the appropriate standard. To date, for example, the SQH has not been made mandatory: it surely must, for it would be irresponsible to make the investment that has been made, ostensibly to enhance the quality of leadership in Scotland's schools, if the SQH did not *qualify* the holder to perform a leadership role. If the aim is merely to extend credentialism, a much less demanding award could have been introduced. The SQH — and the other standards are likely to follow its example — is intended to be academically demanding, but the inclusion of substantial work-based components is intended to provide a measure of advanced professional performance, exactly what a professional qualification should be. The same requirement might well be extended to the other standards.

A second significant approach might be to offer financial incentives for those achieving particular professional standards. Already, arrangements of this kind are under discussion south of the border. The McCrone Committee was established in 1999 to consider "how teachers' pay, promotion structures, and conditions of service should be changed in order to ensure a committed, professional and flexible teaching force which will secure high and improving standards of education for all children in Scotland into the new Millennium..." It is not inconceivable that the McCrone Committee might recommend that CPD achievements should be rewarded by higher pay.

While these two measures might benefit those who seek promotion and career advancement of one kind or another, they would not make CPD an integral feature of the life of every teacher. A third approach is necessary to achieve that objective: that is, in addition to the two measures described, to make participation in CPD a condition of continued registration with the GTC.

The Role of the GTC in CPD

The original establishment of the GTC was a direct response to the employment of unqualified teachers: it was a mechanism for protecting standards of admission to the profession. Not surprisingly, since the continuing professional development of teachers was not then considered to be a matter of importance, the legislation restricted the powers of the GTC to teachers' final registration at the end of the probationary period, although it did confer on the GTC the right to remove from the register teachers whose conduct was judged to be unprofessional. Recognising that the quality of the teaching force is not to be secured simply by the rigorous scrutiny of academic and professional credentials at the point of entry, the GTC has, over the years, campaigned to have its powers extended to enable it to secure a locus in the CPD of teachers. The election of a Labour government in 1997, with its manifesto commitment to enhancing the status and standing of teaching, raised expectations. These were raised even higher when the government's white paper (SEED, 1999) indicated that it intended to consider an extension of the powers of the GTC to enable it perhaps to deregister teachers who had been dismissed for incompetence, to entitle it to advise Scottish ministers on the framing of standards for CPD, and perhaps also to accredit in-service programmes. When, in December 1998, the Minister, Helen Liddell, intimated a review of the GTC, she affirmed that the intention was to enable the Council "to strengthen and expand its vital role in raising standards and enhancing professionalism among Scottish teachers in the future". She considered that the GTC "should be a pace-setter for the teaching profession in the 21st century". Such language clearly implied that the extension of the powers of the GTC would form part of the agenda of the review.

And so it proved. The reviewers, Deloitte and Touche (1999b), having tested professional opinion and compared the functions of the GTC with other similar bodies, made a number of important recommendations. Firstly, they proposed that the GTC should have the ability to deregister a teacher who had been dismissed by an employer. That is, the GTC would determine whether the grounds for dismissal were sufficiently severe to warrant removal from the register. The GTC's locus in the handling of incompetence cases has been criticised as inappropriate for a body dominated by teachers and as an unacceptable infringement of the responsibilities of those who employ teachers. The GTC's response to these criticisms is three-fold. Firstly, it has long experience of deregistering those found guilty of professional misconduct. Secondly, its whole credibility as a professional body is weakened because it does not have the authority to remove those from the register judged to be incompetent. Thirdly, it has distinguished between dismissal and deregistration: it has maintained that it is inappropriate for a teacher who is dismissed for incompetence by one authority to find employment with another. The Deloitte Touche recommendation, which would entitle the GTC to deregister a teacher after (s)he had been dismissed for incompetence, solves this particular boundary dispute. For its part, the SEED (2000) has accepted that recommendation and has indicated its intention to legislate to that effect. Of course, given that the number of teachers thought to be incompetent is likely to be small, no-one expects that that measure alone will decisively affect the well-being and quality of the profession. Further measures are clearly called for and the Deloitte Touche review recommended accordingly.

Again reflecting the consensus revealed in the survey, the reviewers concluded that there were several functions relating to the CPD of teachers that should fall within the responsibility of the GTC. These included:

advising teacher employers and the Scottish Office "on a framework of competences spanning all levels of the teaching profession, as a foundation for CPD";
commissioning research on the identification of training needs;
maintaining teachers' CPD records on the register.

The SEED has accepted these recommendations.

There were, however, two matters which the reviewers considered but judged it inappropriate to introduce at present. The first of these concerns the accreditation of CPD provision. The GTC has long argued that its experience of accrediting initial teacher education programmes provides a perfectly sound basis for performing that same function with regard to CPD. Indeed, the Council's effectiveness as the custodian of professional standards is limited if it has no locus in evaluating CPD provision. The reviewers acknowledged that it would be entirely appropriate to place responsibility for CPD accreditation with "a body which could take a dispassionate view (not being itself a provider) on an all-Scotland basis". Despite that, they were unable to recommend that the Council's powers be extended in this way, apparently on the unconvincing grounds that for the GTC to assume responsibility for accrediting CPD would be "labour-intensive".

The second issue recommended for deferral was the establishment of an "active" register, which would require "evidence of satisfactory CPD on the part of professional teachers in order to justify their continuing registration with the GTC". Here, the case for deferral rested on more credible grounds. Experience in other professional domains — significantly including the very professional body which is concerned with professional and personnel development — suggested that it was wise to proceed "cautiously" in this area. Besides, the establishment of an active register would create an entitlement to CPD opportunities which most authorities would find it impossible to satisfy. Forrester (1999) has also drawn attention to the legal minefield that is to be encountered when a teacher threatened with deregistration offers the defence that (s)he had been denied opportunities by the employer. For these and similar reasons, Deloitte Touche considered that a decision on the active register should be deferred. SEED has accepted this recommendation, agreeing that accreditation and the active register should be reconsidered once the other tasks are bedded into the GTC's work. (SEED, 1999)

SEED's acceptance of the Deloitte Touche recommendations is regrettable. While it is gratifying that the GTC will have a locus in CPD, that role is unnecessarily restricted. There is no doubt that the GTC is now equipped to accredit CPD provision and the failure to extend the Council's role in this way, while at the same time recognising its role in the accreditation of ITE, simply perpetuates an anomaly. No doubt, there are strong prudential grounds for deferring a decision on the active register, for there are likely to be serious political difficulties in making registration conditional on the completion of CPD activities, even if the resources were available on the scale required. Nevertheless, the active register is perhaps the key to the revitalisation of CPD, not least because it establishes an entitlement to access to appropriate opportunities. If time is needed to create the necessary conditions for an active register, a declaration could have been made at the time of the review of the GTC that the active register would be introduced within a specified timescale. That would have been an appropriate decision by a government that saw CPD as vital to the health of the profession and the quality of teaching and learning in schools. SEED has carefully dodged the consultants' precise recommendation that the matter should be deferred for a five-year period. Nevertheless, the form of words chosen could be interpreted as a recipe for indefinite postponement of a change that is fundamental.

CHAPTER 5

QUALITY ASSURANCE

Introduction

The quality of any educational service depends pre-eminently on the quality of its teachers. The more education is seen as the key to economic prosperity, to the well-being of the community, and to all kinds of individual and human flourishing, the more vital it is to ensure that teachers are of the highest quality and have the expertise, resourcefulness and commitment that will enable them to discharge ever more demanding responsibilities. Previous chapters have considered ways in which still further enhancements in the quality of teachers are to be secured: by integrating teacher education into the research environment of universities, and enabling teachers at the beginning of and throughout their careers to access the intellectual resources of these institutions; by establishing a national standard for the beginning teacher, consisting of a set of competences which reflect the complexity of teaching in the contemporary context; by adjusting the framework of teaching qualifications to accord with curricular and other educational changes; by strengthening partnership with teachers in schools to ensure that students' off-campus learning is subject to the same quality assurance requirements as university-based studies; and by establishing a framework of standards for the continuing professional development of teachers which guarantees that teachers are professionally qualified to undertake new roles and responsibilities and are able, if not required, to revitalise their skills and knowledge continuously throughout their careers.

In addition to seeking such improvements in provision, educational institutions, not least those responsible for the education and professional development of teachers, have an obligation to demonstrate how the quality of the educational experience they provide and the standards achieved by their students are being maintained and enhanced: they are expected to have in place quality assurance arrangements which are sufficiently robust to generate professional and public confidence in their work.

In recent years all institutions of higher education have been required to be more accountable in this sense and have been subjected to forms of external scrutiny that are unprecedented in their scope and intensity. Moreover, a welter of further changes are being prepared for implementation at the start of session 2000/2001 which will have a transformational effect on the life of institutions of higher education and the ways in which they assure the quality of their work. This chapter outlines the established approaches to quality assurance, and it assesses the new and more stringent procedures that are being introduced across higher education as a whole, together with the additional requirements being imposed on teacher education institutions.

Quality Assurance Arrangements in Higher Education

All institutions of higher education have adopted quality assurance arrangements which fall into two categories: internal and external. While these are related, they are nevertheless worth differentiating in order to demonstrate the extensiveness of the commitment institutions of higher education are expected to invest in the assurance of quality.

The first of the internal features relates to the *selection of students*. One of the important characteristics of strong programmes is that they have rigorous selection procedures. Over the years, there has been a progressive raising of entrance qualifications for admission to teaching. The actual requirements are set out annually in a government *Memorandum* which is binding on all institutions. Since all teacher education programmes lead to university awards, the minimum entrance qualifications are those which relate to admission to a university. However, in addition, the national guidelines for teacher education programmes stipulate that the selection process should include face-to-face interaction in order to identify from the large number of applicants those judged most suited to teaching. The assumption is that the selection of candidates for a professional activity such as teaching should certainly take account of scholastic achievements, but should also seek to assess potential students' capacity to communicate with others, to interact with colleagues, and the strength of their commitment to teaching.

Secondly, high quality programmes depend on the *selection of appropriate staff*. Statutorily, those engaged on courses relating to the theory and practice of teaching must themselves be registered with the General Teaching Council. Of course, that is a minimal condition for appointment. At all teacher education institutions the aim is to recruit members of staff who are accomplished teachers, and it is usual to admit to the staff of TEIs those who have substantial experience of working in schools, who show evidence of engagement in research and development activities, and who have played a key role in professional development activities in school settings or as members of national and local curriculum development groups.

Thirdly, the quality of a programme depends on the rigorous scrutiny of an academic *approval process* before it is offered. It is standard practice for a development group to be established, consisting of staff, practising teachers and student representatives, to undertake the necessary planning and to bring forward a programme proposal. The documentation generated to support the proposal usually involves the following:

(a) evidence of need
(b) rationale
(c) aims and curriculum
(d) teaching and learning strategies
(e) assessment
(f) compatibility with ITE *Guidelines*, professional expectations and university standards
(g) arrangements for partnership with schools
(h) resources
(i) course management and quality assurance arrangements.

Normally, a programme proposal is scrutinised intensively by a small group drawn from different parts of the institution and, in line with the national guidelines, consisting of external members drawn from another university as well as from the teaching profession. It is then subjected to further scrutiny by at least one other university-wide committee before being formally approved as a programme leading to a university award, prior to its submission for external approval.

Fourthly, all programmes are subjected to regular *evaluation on an annual basis*. Normally, responsibility for the academic health of a programme is placed with a programme committee, again consisting of teaching staff, practising teachers and students, and led by a programme leader. Such committees are charged to undertake regular evaluation of the programme and to submit an annual report covering the following:

(a) cohort analysis (from the number of applicants to the percentage completing)
(b) measure of client satisfaction
(c) measure of academic effectiveness (for example, non-completion rate, distribution of Honours awards)
(d) feedback from tutors and schools
(e) formal response to report of external examiner(s)
(f) recommended changes and adjustments in the light of the discussion generated by the evidence in (a) to (e) above.

Again, it is normal practice for the annual programme evaluation report to be submitted to a committee such as an Undergraduate Studies Committee or the Faculty Board, so that it can be considered by a wider group of staff.

Fifthly, all programmes are subjected from time to time to *review*. A review differs from annual evaluation in the sense that it implies periodicity: it makes possible the analysis of the total experience of a programme over a number of years. There are two classical review questions:

Has the programme been achieving its objectives?
Are the objectives still valid, or do they require modification in the light of institutional, professional and other developments?

In addressing these questions, review documentation is expected to cover the following:

(a) the validation and accreditation history of the programme
(b) the review process and its agenda
(c) the cumulative reports of external examiners and institutional responses;
(d) analysis of institutional, professional and other developments pointing to the need for change
(e) the revised programme, covering aims, curriculum, teaching strategies and assessments
(f) measures to maintain the health of the programme, particularly in the face of intensifying resource constraints.

Again, it is usual for review panels to include members drawn from other parts of the institution, as well as external members.

Finally, it is usual for institutions to establish a mechanism — an Academic Standards Committee or an Audit Committee — with responsibility for ensuring that the quality assurance arrangements are operating as they should. *Auditing* is a second order function: it does not itself involve programme evaluation or review: rather, it seeks to ensure that institutional expectations with regard to the maintenance of quality are met. It is common for audit committees or their equivalent to carry out their work by sampling institutional procedures, and by conducting audit trails, which issue in reports to the academic board or senate on the extent to which the stated institutional procedures are being adhered to. For example, an audit trail might test the extent to which a programme committee is responding appropriately to reports by external examiners. It is also common for audit committees to have a role in disseminating good practice throughout an institution.

In addition to these various forms of internal appraisal and analysis, all programmes are subjected to several forms of external scrutiny, also intended to test the quality of the educational experience offered and the standards of awards. The first of these is the *external examining* system. Its underlying assumption is that standards are maintained by requiring universities to appoint from other institutions one or more people of standing and experience in each field of study to approve the assessment arrangements, to scrutinise the assessments made of students' work, to testify that the standard of awards conforms to the UK norm, and to challenge an institution to ensure that each of its programmes is in line with the best provision elsewhere.

Secondly, the Funding Councils, when they were instituted in the early 1990s, established *teaching quality assessment* (TQA), a process by which provision in each area of work in an institution of higher education was scrutinised by an external group "to provide a basis for advice to Council on the quality of educational provision in higher education institutions funded by the Scottish Higher Education Funding Council (SHEFC)". A quality assessment framework was developed covering aims and curricula; curriculum design and review; the teaching and learning environment; staff resources; learning resources; course organisation; teaching and learning practice; student support; assessment and monitoring; students' work; outputs and quality control. Institutions were assessed on each of these areas and an overall judgement made on a four-point scale as follows:

> Excellent
> Highly Satisfactory
> Satisfactory
> Unsatisfactory.

These judgements and the reports from which they were derived were made public. In this way, maximum pressure was exerted on institutions to achieve high ratings, particularly when there were financial rewards for achieving a rating of Excellent, and when an Unsatisfactory rating could lead to the threat of withdrawal of funding.

The third form of external scrutiny consists of *quality audit*, previously undertaken by the Higher Education Quality Council (HEQC). Again, a group of trained external auditors undertook a detailed scrutiny of an institution to test the robustness of its quality assurance arrangements, and a public report was generated identifying areas of strength and weakness and where institutional action was required. Whereas, therefore, teaching quality assessment sought to establish the effectiveness of provision in a particular domain of academic activity, quality audit provided a comprehensive analysis of how an institution assured the standards and quality of its work.

Fourthly, teacher education institutions had to submit their programmes for *approval by the Secretary of State for Scotland*. The justification for that arrangement was that the Secretary of State could not exercise responsibility for the quality of education in schools unless he controlled the nature of teacher education. The Secretary of State discharged that responsibility by promulgating national guidelines for teacher education courses and stipulating that one of the criteria for the approval of a programme was that it was compatible with the national guidelines.

The fifth form of external scrutiny concerned *accreditation by the General Teaching Council for Scotland*. Since the GTC is the body which formally admits a person to the teaching profession, it has to be able to satisfy itself that programmes are professionally acceptable. The GTC exercises this responsibility by visiting institutions from time to time to study particular areas of provision, and also by accrediting programmes when they are first introduced, and subjecting them subsequently to periodic review, normally every five years.

Finally, the Teaching and Higher Education Act (1998) reintroduced the right of the Secretary of State to arrange for the periodic *inspection* of TEIs. It was frequently claimed that, once a programme had been approved by the Secretary of State, usually on the advice of members of the Inspectorate, he had no further way of checking that the work undertaken in the colleges was actually in line with the specification that had been approved and that courses took account of changes of emphasis in the school curriculum. The reinstatement of inspection was thought to remedy that weakness.

These multiple forms of external programme and institutional appraisal served to reinforce sharper levels of self-scrutiny within institutions. Indeed, the overlap and duplication that was inevitably involved was seen as a strength: the greater the range of forms of scrutiny, the less likelihood was there that institutional malpractice would remain undetected. Institutions were therefore pressurised not only to achieve high standards, but also to be accountable for the ways in which these standards were protected and the quality of provision maintained and enhanced.

The New Quality Assurance Arrangements for Higher Education

The re-thinking of approaches to quality assurance was stimulated by the Dearing Report of 1997. The terms of reference of that committee of inquiry required it to adopt an expansionist philosophy of "maximum participation in initial higher education". At the same time, it had to ensure that "standards of degrees and other higher education qualifications should be at least maintained, and assured". That is, the expansion had to be achieved without any erosion of standards or any diminution in the quality of the higher education experience. Reviewing the current position with regard to quality and standards, the committee found grounds for disquiet: the system of external examinations alone was judged incapable of guaranteeing comparability of standards; employers had a "low level of confidence" in the standard of awards; there was "no consistent rationale for the structure and nomenclature of awards across higher education"; the significant increase in the proportion of graduates receiving first or upper second class Honours degrees suggested that "it was not plausible to say that standards had not declined"; there was a significant body of opinion in higher education itself which held that at the broad subject level "little precise comparability of standards exists"; and, finally, the report quoted the evidence it had received from the Higher Education Quality Council (HEQC) itself:

> The Council's work does make it clear that the consequence of current changes in higher education is that traditional understandings of what a degree is no longer hold good ... Essential aspects of the academic infrastructure that used to support confidence in shared standards have been undermined, with resultant problems of understanding for students, employers, research councils, and academics themselves, since the existing frames of reference no longer match reality. (Dearing, 1997)

That assessment was bound to be taken as authoritative, coming as it did from the very body which saw itself as the custodian of standards in higher education.

The Funding Councils relied on teaching quality assessment (TQA) to raise the profile of teaching and to encourage universities to be much more preoccupied with the learning experience of their students. Dearing was also strongly critical of TQA:

> Given that the vast majority of outcomes have been satisfactory, we are not convinced that it would be the best use of scarce resources to continue the system in the long-term. Moreover, we believe that it is exceedingly difficult for the TQA process to review the quality of learning and teaching itself, rather than proxies for learning and teaching, such as available resources or lecture presentation. The utility of such a system is also likely to wane as institutions 'learn' how to achieve high ratings. (Dearing, 1997)

Dearing maintained that, if the "qualified trust" between higher education institutions and their stakeholders was to be restored, radical changes were required. These included:

> a framework of qualifications based on agreed credits and levels of achievement;
> recognised standards of awards, based on benchmark information in each domain of study;
> a learning experience for students which enabled them to meet the standards of the award;
> clear and accurate information for students, employers and others about the content, standards and delivery of programmes;
> the establishment of national codes of practice to support quality provision covering all aspects of academic and institutional life.

The Sutherland Report on teacher education was also critical of quality assurance arrangements. It reflected a widespread consensus that there were too many separate levels of external scrutiny and that there would be advantage in a certain degree of streamlining.

The recommendations of the Dearing Committee led to an extensive development programme by the Quality Assurance Agency for Higher Education (QAAHE), involving wide consultation and the trialling of the principal features of the new model. The first of these is the *qualifications framework*. To combat the inconsistencies in nomenclature and in the length of programmes leading to the same titled award, Dearing recommended the introduction of a framework "to ensure that qualifications that share a common title are of a common level and nature". (QAA, 1998) Such a framework will also facilitate credit accumulation and transfer, and help to systematise lifelong learning opportunities. While the definitive statement on the qualifications framework has not yet been produced, it is very likely that the framework in Scotland will have six levels, each with a credit rating expressed as Scottish Degree (SD) points or Scottish Master's (SM) points:

Qualification	Credit Rating
Certificate of Higher Education	120 SD points
Diploma of Higher Education	240 SD points
Ordinary/General Degree	360 SD points
Bachelor's Degree with Honours	480 SD points
Master's Degrees	180 SM points
Doctorates	No credit rating

Moreover, it is expected that in Scotland there will be a further differentiation, in line with practice in the teacher education institutions: a postgraduate certificate (60 SM credit points) and a postgraduate diploma (120 SM credit points) will represent the first two phases of the Master's Degree.

The second area for development work concerns *programme specification*. The aim here is "to help institutions set out clearly the intended outcomes of their programmes of study". (QAA, 1998) Each programme will be expected to state explicitly the objectives of the programme outcomes, its content, and the ways in which the attainment of the programme objectives will be assessed. Institutions would be expected, for each programme, to set out, for example,

knowledge, understanding and skills;
teaching and learning strategies;
assessment methods by which learners' achievements will be demonstrated;
the relationship of the programme to the appropriate qualifications framework.

Thirdly, again following the Dearing recommendation, it is proposed to introduce in each subject area agreed *national benchmark standards*. The aim is "to produce broad statements which represent general expectations about standards for the award of an Honours degree in a particular subject area..." (QAA, 1999) Benchmarking seeks to describe "the intellectual capability and understanding that should be developed through the study of that discipline to Honours degree level; the techniques and skills which are associated with developing understanding in that discipline; and the level of intellectual demand and challenge which is appropriate to Honours degree subjects in that discipline". While some have detected in the benchmarking exercise the beginnings of a common higher education curriculum in each of the different subject domains, the QAA has maintained that consistency of standards is impossible to determine unless there is agreement within each academic subject community on those achievements which should represent Honours level work in its domain.

Finally, *codes of practice* are being developed which set out what is assumed to be good academic practice in all areas of the academic life of an institution. These will cover admissions; careers guidance; distance learning; external examiners; postgraduate research; programme specification, design and approval; and staff recruitment, training and development. Taken together, these codes of practice should represent a set of standards against which provision in any institution might be judged.

The recommendations made by the Sutherland Report were taken forward by a working party chaired by the Secretary of the Scottish Office Education and Industry Department (SOEID). In an endeavour to streamline quality assurance arrangements that committee recommended that all the internal quality assurance mechanisms should be retained and, indeed, that practices should be made more consistent across all TEIs. In addition, it proposed that the external forms of scrutiny should be combined into what was called *"collaborative review"*. Every six years each teacher education institution would be scrutinised by an external group consisting of representatives from the General Teaching Council, the Inspectorate, and the Quality Assurance Agency. While these three agencies might have certain interests in common, they will also have areas of specific concern. Thus, the Quality Assurance Agency might wish to assess the extent to which institutional practices comply with the advice set out in the various codes of practice; the Inspectorate might be concerned about the amount of attention devoted, for example, to reading and the development of literacy in primary education programmes; while the GTC might wish to interrogate an institution's partnership arrangements with schools. Clearly, collaborative review will call for an unprecedented degree of co-operation between these three bodies and further work will be required to establish precisely what collaborative review will entail. Accordingly, a further working party has been established, chaired by a senior member of the Inspectorate, to establish the detailed operational arrangements for collaborative review. A central feature of that work will involve the development of benchmark statements for initial teacher education based, in all probability, on the statement of competences already in operation.

Finally, in addition to these arrangements, the Inspectorate have retained the right to undertake periodically — as ministers appear to require — "aspect" reports on particular areas of provision. For example, there is current concern about standards of literacy in Scottish schools and it would be reasonable for ministers to request the Inspectorate to report on a matter of that kind. In compiling that report, the Inspectorate might well wish to undertake a study of provision made for teaching of literacy in the TEIs.

The New Reporting Process

Each institution will participate in a cycle of reviews over a six-year period in the course of which each subject area will be scrutinised and a summative assessment made of the effectiveness of the institution's overall arrangements for the management of quality assurance. The fundamental aim behind this integrated process of institutional scrutiny is "to ensure public confidence that quality and standards are being safeguarded, to provide public information, to meet the statutory responsibilities of the funding bodies, and to help institutions enhance the quality of their provision". (QAA, 1999)

The reporting of an institution's quality assurance arrangements will cover three areas. Firstly, there will be a report which is concerned with the *institutional management of standards and quality*. That report will evaluate the arrangements made by institutions for programme approval and review, and seek to assess their adherence to the various codes of practice. The purpose of this institution-wide scrutiny is to determine the extent to which confidence can be placed in an institution's capacity to maintain standards and the robustness of its mechanisms to ensure that these standards are being maintained.

Secondly, there will be a report concerned with *programme outcome standards*. The aim will be to determine the extent to which there are specified learning outcomes for each programme which reflect the national subject benchmarks at the required level. It will cover such matters as the design of the curriculum; assessment strategies; and the level of achievement of students.

Thirdly, a report will be produced on "the quality of the *learning opportunities* in each domain". That will cover *teaching and learning* (the effectiveness and variety of the teaching and learning strategies); *student progression* (the pattern of recruitment, forms of academic support and progression within the programme, and non-completion); and *learning resources* (the effectiveness of the equipment, the use of accommodation, library and computer provision, and the academic and professional expertise of staff).

The format of the report on the quality of learning opportunities provided by institutions has proved controversial. In higher education as a whole there would have been a preference for the avoidance of summative assessments, such as "Excellent" or "Highly Satisfactory", on the grounds that the use of such terms leads too easily to the establishment of "unfair" or "meaningless" league tables. Accordingly, institutions expressed a strong preference for verbally elaborated descriptions of quality of provision and for the avoidance of any kind of summative judgement. However, under pressure from the Funding Council and others, the QAA proposed that each of the three aspects — teaching and learning, student progression, and learning resources — will be categorised as "commendable", "approved", or "failing". Naturally, it would be open to the Funding Councils, if they wished, to conclude that an institution where outcome standards were appropriate and which achieved three ratings of "commendable" could be judged overall to have reached the equivalent of the former rating of Excellent and, therefore, was worthy of recognition through additional funding.

Whatever the shortcomings or merits of the proposed new reporting arrangements, at least they overcome the difficulty that characterised the arrangements now to be superseded: in England only three summative categories were used — Excellent, Satisfactory, and Unsatisfactory — whereas in Scotland there were four: Excellent, Highly Satisfactory, Satisfactory, and Unsatisfactory. Naturally, fewer Excellent ratings were made in Scotland, since reviewers could have recourse to another rating other than Satisfactory. Unfortunately, when university league tables came to be compiled, there was concern in Scottish political circles that Scotland was not achieving as many Excellent ratings as institutions south of the border, and there was a concern that that might denote genuine differences in quality, rather than reflect inconsistencies in the rating systems deployed. The new arrangements will mean that all institutions of higher education in the UK will have their teaching assessed on the same basis.

Not all members of the higher education community have welcomed these developments. For some, they are thought to be a tiresome piece of bureaucracy; for others, they constitute a misuse of scarce resources; and for others still, they constitute a distraction from the central purposes of an institution of higher education. In the words of one critic,

> Since the mid-1980s a pervasive managerial culture has been imposed upon us. The justification was to promote excellence in teaching and research ... Bureaucratisation has not fostered excellence: the university has not become more open, flexible or creative; on the contrary, innovation has been stifled and professional autonomy eroded. Worse still, the pressure to standardise university life has diverted academic time towards the endless round of repetitive paperwork in order to meet the expanding needs of agencies auditing teaching and research. (Furedi, 2000)

Nevertheless, the political pressure on the higher education system has been such that the QAA has pursued the new policy energetically to the point where the institutions themselves realise that there is no escape from the new disciplines and forms of external scrutiny that are now being put in place. The Chair of the Committee of Vice-Chancellors and Principals, Howard Newby, is widely quoted as remarking that what was being introduced was "not a system the universities would have devised left to their own devices". Another critic, Baty (2000), reported that "83% of the 96 institutions that responded to the consultation paper said they did not believe that the reporting format outlined in the consultation paper — and now adopted almost in its entirety — was adequate". However, those who are concerned about the level of public funding attracted by higher education believe that this intensification of accountability is inevitable and see in the new arrangements a way in which institutions will be forced to pay even more careful attention to the development of programmes, to teaching and learning, and to the ways in which standards are to be maintained.

Conclusion

The new quality assurance model and the new approach to reporting will also apply to teacher education institutions and faculties of education. Following, as they do, the recommendations of Dearing and Sutherland, the new arrangements are expected to intensify institutional accountability: the more extensive public reporting on performance at subject and institutional levels is expected to create an even more powerful stimulus to improved institutional performance.

There is a tendency in the public discussion of education in Scotland and elsewhere for teachers to be harshly criticised for whatever shortcomings are detected in schools. Indeed, teacher educators often attract even more opprobrium. The community needs to be assured that standards of teacher education are indeed improving and that the quality assurance arrangements necessary to protect these standards are securely in place. The first four chapters of this book have sought to show that over the last decade significant changes have been made to enhance the quality of provision. They have argued that more changes are required if teacher education institutions are to move further up the ramp of quality. The developments described in the present chapter demonstrate the lengths to which the higher educational community as a whole must go to ensure that standards are high and are being maintained. The rigour of the internal and external scrutiny of programmes and the institutions in which these are embedded should ensure that the pressure to seek still further improvements will intensify. It is perhaps one of the hallmarks of a strong system that it has the capacity to respond positively to such pressures.

REFERENCES

Baty, P, (2000), "Over 80% vetoed blueprint", *The Times Higher Education Supplement*, 28 January 2000, page 9

Brown, S, (1996), "School-based Initial Teacher Education in Scotland: Archaic Highlands or High Moral Ground?" in *Teacher Education Policy: Some issues arising from research and practice*, edited by McBride, R, The Falmer Press, London

Cameron-Jones, M, and O'Hara, P, (1993), *The Scottish Pilot PGCE (Secondary) Course 1992–1993*, Moray House Institute of Education, August 1993, Edinburgh

Cameron-Jones, M, and O'Hara, P, (1994), *The Second Year 1993–94 of the Scottish Pilot PGCE (Secondary) Course*, Moray House Institute of Education, Edinburgh

Cameron-Jones, M, and O'Hara, P, (1997), "Comparisons of newly qualified teachers past and present", in *Scottish Educational Review*, Vol 29, No 1

Carr, D, (1993), "Guidelines for Teacher Training: the competency model" in *Scottish Educational Review*, 25, No 1, pp 17–25

Casteel, V, Forde, C, Reeves, J, and Lynas R, (1997), *A Framework for Leadership and Management Development in Scottish Schools*, QIE, University of Strathclyde, Glasgow

Dearing, Sir R, (1997), *Higher Education in the Learning Society: Report of the National Committee of Inquiry*, HMSO, Norwich, Chapter 10, pp 155, 157

Deloitte and Touche, (1999a), *Costs of Partnership in Initial Teacher Education*, Final Report to the Scottish Office Education and Industry Department and the General Teaching Council for Scotland, Edinburgh

Deloitte and Touche, (1999b), *Review of the General Teaching Council for Scotland: Final Report*, Edinburgh

Draper, J, Fraser, H, Raab, A, Sharp, S, and Taylor, W, (1997), *Routes into Primary Teaching*, Moray House Institute of Education, Edinburgh

Draper, J, Fraser, H, and Taylor, W, (1997), "Teachers at Work: early experiences of professional development" in *British Journal of In-service Education*, Vol. 23, No 2

Forrester, F, (1999), "Should teachers' careers be registered?", *The Times Educational Supplement Scotland*, 24 September 1999, page 7

Furedi, F, (2000), "A wake-up call for all", *The Times Higher Education Supplement*, 28 January 2000, page 20

Furlong, J, Whitty G, Whiting C, Miles, S, Barton, L, and Barrett, E, (1996), "Redefining Partnership: Revolution or Reform in Initial Teacher Education" in *Journal of Education for Teaching*, Vol 22, No 1, pp 39–55

General Teaching Council for Scotland, The, (1997), *The Report of the Working Group on Partnership in Initial Teacher Education*, March 1997, paragraph 6.2.3

Holmes Group, The, (1986), *Tomorrow's Teachers*, East Lansing, USA

Holmes Group, The, (1995), *Tomorrow's Schools*, East Lansing, USA, pp 1/2, 81

Humes, W M, (1995), "From Disciplines to Competencies: the changing face of professional studies in teacher education" in *Education in the North*, New Series, No 3, pp 39–47

Humes, W M, (1995), "Responsibility without power: the management of mentoring". Proceedings of the Annual Conference of the Scottish Educational Research Association

Kirk, G, (1984), Personal submission to the Scottish Tertiary Education Advisory Council

Kirk, G, (1985), "The Future Context of Professional Education" in *Moray House and Professional Education*, Scottish Academic Press, Edinburgh, Chapter 15

Kirk, G, (1995), "Teacher Education: Changing Partnerships" in *Collaborate or Compete? Educational partnerships in a market economy*, edited by Macbeath, A, McCreath, D, and Aitchison, J, Falmer Press, London, Chapter 10, page 117

Kirk, G, (1996), "Partnership: The sharing of cultures?" in *Partnership and Cooperation*. Papers from the 21st Annual Conference of the Association for Teacher Education in Europe (ATEE), University of Strathclyde, Glasgow

Kirk, G, (1997), "Teacher Education" in *A Future for Higher Education in Scotland*, edited by Crawford, R L, Committee of Scottish Higher Education Principals, Chapter 13

Kirk, G, (1997), *The Scottish Tertiary Education Advisory Council: A Case Study in Educational Policy-making*, PhD Thesis, The Open University

Kirk, G, (1999), "The Passing of Monotechnic Teacher Education in Scotland" in *Scottish Educational Review*, Vol 31, No 2, November 1999

Macintyre, D, (1994), "Classrooms as learning environments for beginning teachers" in *Collaboration and Transition in Initial Teacher Training*, edited by Wilkin, M, and Sankey, D, Cogan Page, London

Marker, W, (1999), "The Professional Development of Teachers" in *Scottish Education*, edited by Bryce, T G K, and Humes, W M, Edinburgh University Press, page 924

North Lanarkshire Council, Education Committee paper, (1999), *The curriculum of the Secondary School*

Powney, J, Edward, S, Holroyd, C, and Martin, S, (1993), *Monitoring the Pilot: The Moray House Institute PGCE (Secondary)*, Scottish Council for Research in Education, Edinburgh, November 1993

Quality Assurance Agency for Higher Education, The, (1998), *Higher Quality*, No 4, October 1998, page 4

Quality Assurance Agency for Higher Education, The, (1999), *Higher Quality*, No 5, May 1999, page 4

Quality Assurance Agency for Higher Education, The, (1999), *Higher Quality*, No 6, November 1999, page 3

Scottish Consultative Council on the Curriculum, (1999), *Curriculum Design for the Secondary Stages, Guidelines for Schools*, Edinburgh

Scottish Education Department, (1946), *Training of Teachers: A Report of the Advisory Council on Education in Scotland*, HMSO, Edinburgh, Command 6723

Scottish Education Department, (1985), *Future Strategy for Higher Education in Scotland (STEAC Report)*, HMSO, Edinburgh,

Scottish Education Department, (1988), *Review of Teacher Training at the University of Stirling*, HMSO, Edinburgh

Scottish Executive Education Department, (1999), *Improving our schools: Consultation on the General Teaching Council for Scotland*, Edinburgh

Scottish Executive Education Department, (1999), *New Community Schools Prospectus*, Edinburgh

Scottish Executive Education Department, (1999), *Targetting Excellence — Modernising Scotland's Schools*, Edinburgh

Scottish Executive Education Department, (2000), *Improving our Schools: consultation response*, Edinburgh

Scottish Higher Education Funding Council, (1995), *Teaching Quality Assessment of Initial Teacher Education*, Edinburgh

Scottish Office Education and Industry Department, (1998), *The Standard for Headship in Scotland*, June 1998, Edinburgh

Scottish Office Education and Industry Department, (1998), *Guidelines for Initial Teacher Education Courses in Scotland*, Edinburgh

Scottish Office Education and Industry Department, (1998), Consultation paper on *A National Framework for the Continuing Professional Development of Teachers*, Edinburgh

Scottish Office Education and Industry Department, (1998), *The Scottish Qualification for Headship Programme*, October 1998, Edinburgh

Scottish Office Education and Industry Department, (1999), *Standards and Quality in Scottish Schools: 1995–1998*, A report by HM Inspectors of Schools, Edinburgh

Scottish Office Education Department, (1993), *Guidelines for teacher training courses*, Edinburgh

Scottish Office Education Department, (1993), *Report of SOED Seminar on Partnership Initiatives in Initial Teacher Training*, 16/17 November 1993, The Scottish Office, Edinburgh

Scottish Office Education Department, (1993), *The Structure and Balance of the curriculum 5-14*, Edinburgh

Stark, R, (1994), "The giving can't go on", *The Times Educational Supplement*, 18 February 1994

Stronach, I, Cope, P, Inglis, B, McNally, J, (1994), "The SOED Competence Guidelines for Initial Teacher Training: issues of control, performance and relevance" in *Scottish Educational Review*, Vol 26, No 2, November

Sutherland, Sir S, (1997), "Teacher Education and Training: A Study", Report 10 of *Higher Education in the Learning society* (Dearing: National Committee of Inquiry into Higher Education), HMSO, Norwich

Universities' Funding Council, (1991), *Criteria for assessing merger proposals from institutions of higher education in Scotland*, Report of Scottish Committee, Edinburgh

Wilkin, M, (1999), *The Role of Higher Education in Initial Teacher Education*, Occasional Paper 2, Universities Council for the Education of Teachers, London, January 1999